Human Values in the Classroom

Human Values in the Classroom

A Handbook for Teachers

Robert C. Hawley
Isabel L. Hawley

Hart Publishing Company, Inc. · New York City

CONTENTS

ACKNOWLEDGMENTS   7

Part I: Human Values and Education

  1. Human Values and Education   13

Part II: A Sequence of Teaching Concerns

  2. Where to Begin   33
  3. Orientation   45
  4. Community Building   50
  5. Achievement Motivation   83
  6. Fostering Open Communication   102
  7. Information Seeking, Gathering and
         Sharing   135
  8. Value Exploration and Clarification   145
  9. Planning for Change   206

*Part III: Notes on Teaching for Personal and
     Social Growth*

10. Positive Focus   223
11. Grades and Evaluation   236

12. Discipline and Behavior Control   253

Part IV: Appendixes

A. An Approach to Inter-Disciplinary
        Problems   259
B. A Conversation Among Teachers   261
C. Suggestions for Further Reading   267

INDEX   273

INDEX OF ACTIVITIES   281

ACKNOWLEDGMENTS

Tracing personal growth activities to their sources is almost as difficult as tracing the sources of jokes or current sayings: they exist in the air and seem to be the product of spontaneous generation. Indeed, we have often had the experience of "inventing" a new activity to fill a specific need, and later hearing of an almost identical activity being used elsewhere. Activities in this book are attributed to the earliest source that we have been able to find; activities not attributed are untraceable or, to the best of our knowledge, original.

Special acknowledgment goes to Dr. Jeffrey W. Eiseman, especially for simulations, role playing, and laboratory learning; to Dr. Sidney B. Simon, particularly for methods of value clarification; and to Dr. David Britton, whose conception of positive focus in teaching has changed our lives. We wish to thank these three men for their help, their friendship, and their influence.

In addition, we owe a debt of gratitude to our students, whose varying needs and expectations over the years have profoundly influenced our thinking, and to our teaching colleagues who have tried out our approaches and activities and have shared with us their experiences and insights.

ROBERT C. HAWLEY
ISABEL L. HAWLEY

To Betsey and Bobby

Human Values
in the Classroom

Part I
Human Values and Education

Chapter One

HUMAN VALUES AND EDUCATION

This book is about teaching human values in the classroom — values such as love, cooperation, trust, acceptance, joy, dignity, respect for individual differences, compromise, truth, understanding, and reverence. These are the human values that moral philosophers and religious leaders have generally agreed upon through the years. These are the human values that must be taught in the classroom and wherever education goes on. Human values must be taught because they are the key to the survival of the species *homo sapiens.* Teaching human values is teaching survival skills.

If humankind is to last beyond the next century, then the massive competitive value structure in which people see only the parts of the puzzle of global survival must be dismantled and replaced. This value structure, which pits man against man in competition over limited resources, must give way to an understanding that the earth's limited resources must be shared by all if any are to survive. In a society based on human values, man's most precious resource is his fellow man. If the school has a function for the future, it is to teach our young these human values, these survival skills.

Let there be no mistake about what this means for the classroom. There can be no preaching. Just as skill at tennis is learned by playing tennis, skill at interdependence is learned by working interdependently, and skill at love is learned through loving. It is the teacher's role to foster human values by creating learning opportunities where human values will come into play. And, perhaps even more difficult for the teacher, it is also his[1] role to live by the values he is teaching.

HUMAN VALUES AND HUMAN NEEDS

Fortunately for teachers, human values are skills, no less than computation or public speaking: accordingly, they can be learned, with hard work, practice, and perseverance. Yet no skill can be taught in an atmosphere which fails to take account of each student's basic needs for safety, belonging-ness, love, respect, and self-esteem — as well as the individual's needs for information, knowledge, and wisdom. The boredom and alienation which pervade our schools signify a craving for the satisfaction of those basic needs.

It is the school's chief function to fill these needs, and in filling them to produce individuals who cannot be bored: individuals who have too high a regard for themselves and too clear a view of the needs of society to find themselves with nothing to do. It is the school's function to produce individuals who cannot feel isolated in the midst of mankind, who have the ability to seek out and initiate friendships and associations, the understanding to take part in collaborative efforts, the wisdom to ask for and to give love. It is the school's chief function to produce socially-self-actualizing people, to use Abraham Maslow's phrase.

Maslow[2] theorizes that basic human needs fall into certain categories: the physiological needs for food, warmth, and shelter; the need for safety and security; the need for belongingness; the need for love; the need for respect and self-esteem; and the need for self-actualization. These needs form a natural hierarchy of perceived importance to the individual. That is, when the individual is primarily concerned with meeting his physiological needs, he has little time for or even awareness of the higher needs for belongingness or love.

As the lower needs are satisfied with increasing ease, they become less important, and the individual shifts his focus to the next higher need. For instance, when a person customarily feels safe and secure, he ceases to think about it and begins to take his safety for granted. Instead, his energies are directed towards the next step in the hierarchy, gaining belongingness, becoming an accepted member of a group.

And so on up the ladder through the hierarchy of needs until the individual has satisfied all of his basic needs and is able to turn his energies toward social-self-actualization. Maslow uses the term *self-actualization,* but he makes it quite clear that genuine self-actualization is also social in nature. Far from merely "doing his own thing," the self-actualizing person sees himself as a socially meliorative agent. To underscore this point, we affix the word *social* to Maslow's term.

The socially-self-actualizing person is energetic, creative, self-motivating, spontaneous, efficient, and tolerant. He lives life fully, answering to his own inner nature and finding in that nature a call to play a useful part in society. He is acting on a foundation of human values.

Here, then, is the task for the schools: to create

conditions which enable young people to work toward satisfying their basic needs, so that they may grow to social-self-actualization;[3] to inhibit feelings of alienation by providing for belongingness and love; to check boredom by providing for respect and self-esteem. In short, the schools must provide those conditions which promote personal and social growth at all levels. The Sequence of Teaching Concerns presented in Part II of this book is designed to develop a classroom atmosphere in which such growth can and will occur.

CLASSROOM ENVIRONMENT AND THE AUTHORITARIAN PERSONALITY

The school should be a place where each student can develop as an individual and at the same time use his powers to further the larger activities of the group. Unfortunately, as our schools are now set up, most students are trained to develop into rigid, self-interested, and dependent people. Our schools often emphasize passive submission to authority rather than independent thought; conformity rather than diversity; neatness rather than creativity. The schools' exercise of power is often arbitrary rather than responsive to student needs — most demonstrably in the formulation of the curriculum and in determining how and what to grade. Even the loudspeaker system clearly indicates that the school is founded on a hierarchy of authority, with the principal at the top and the student at the bottom. All these facts of school life leave their stamp on the student. All support the values of submission to and dependence on authority.

Consider, for example, the physical space in which we teach. To paraphrase Dr. Harold Gores, Director of the Educational Facilities Laboratory of the Ford Foundation, education is a fluid process which pretty much conforms to the space assigned to it. Where our classrooms are shoeboxes lined up neatly along a double-loaded corridor, we tend to think in shoebox terms, putting English in this shoebox, history in that, math in the next; or fifth grade in this shoebox, fourth grade in the box across the hall. It is but a short leap of the imagination to put students into neatly labeled boxes. On the other hand, where the classroom area is a vast open space with no guides or clues as to what learning is likely to go on in what part of the desert, people find it difficult to figure out what they are doing there.

To accommodate human beings who are actively engaged in growing and changing, classrooms need definition and diversity: comfortable, well-lighted places for reading; dark, intimate places for being alone and thinking; informal sitting areas for group discussions; places to be loud and places to be quiet; visually interesting places. In short, young people need rooms for living — living rooms.

There's not much that most teachers can do about the bricks and concrete and plaster that make up their classrooms. Some are limited as to the things that they can put on their walls. Many would risk being fired just by suggesting that the school buy an old armchair, a sofa, or a couple of hassocks to put in their classroom. And the janitor would most likely complain if a teacher brought in an old rug to cover a section of the gray asphalt tile floor.

Yet in some schools, one or another of these things is possible. Teachers can change the climate of their classrooms by introducing an odd piece of living-room furniture or two, by partitioning off a small section of the room with movable bookshelves for a thinking corner, or by setting up a reading area with a couple of old mattresses covered with bright bedspreads and pillows. Many teachers can keep three or four throw rugs or pillows on which students can sit to play games, talk, or read.

Teachers who are unable to do any of these things may at least be able to alter the traditional seating pattern so that the students can sit in a circle, a horseshoe, clusters, or some other informal arrangement. The teacher can abandon his conventional position of authority behind the big desk at the front of the room. And most teachers can introduce some aspects of visual stimulation by bringing collages, mobiles, posters, and other kinds of art and sculpture into the classroom. (Many art museums have special collections for loan to classroom teachers.)

Making the classroom an attractive and comfortable place for human beings — a living room — is not just a nice frill, nor is it a physical manifestation of a permissive, do-your-own-thing and slouch-where-you-please philosophy. The classroom sends messages to the people in the room — messages of safety, security, belongingness, and warmth, messages which say that this is a place where the individual is respected and trusted, where human beings may engage in human activity. In this classroom, learning and living are united.

CREATIVE THINKING

The humane classroom fosters an atmosphere in which true creative thinking can take place. We're not talking here about art and music and poetry and dance and the like. These "creative" arts are already devalued by their minor place in the curriculum. (*Frills* is the general term applied to them in budget meetings.) Art is Tuesday and Thursday from two until three, unless somebody more important shows up, like the Public Health officer. Music is learning the songs that the music teacher likes; poetry is never graded; dance is only for girls. Art and music and poetry and dance *could* be powerful forces in developing creative thinking, but in most instances they have been defused in today's schools.

What we're talking about is creative thinking as it applies to any subject, any area of life. Science, math, history, literature, all are built on the discoveries of creative thinkers. When we examine some of the great creative thinkers — Darwin, Galileo, Beethoven — we discover that their creations were, in reality, making something new out of something old, seeing the little pieces that were already lying around and fitting them together in a new way. Creative thinking is finding the keystone to complete the arch, or turning the world upside down and standing at the perimeter, rather than at the center, of the solar system. If education is seen as the transmission of old knowledge into new heads, then creative thinking has no place. But if education is the systematic encouragement of the human potential to find new ways of living — of surviving — then creative thinking is central to the functioning of the school.

Creative thinking dies in an authoritarian atmosphere, thrives in an atmosphere of psychological freedom and security. When one feels free to speculate, to toy with ideas, to think outrageous and bizarre thoughts, without the threat of lowered self-esteem or the withdrawal of respect, love, friendship, or protection, then one is free to create. When one feels outside forces attempting to control, coerce, limit, or evaluate his thinking, then one feels threatened, and his creative energy is siphoned off into responding to the threat.

Carl Rogers has identified three psychological conditions which foster creativity.[4] The first is *openness to experience,* being continually aware of new perceptions as they come in. Instead of seeing things in predetermined categories ("Grass is green." "Going to church is good." "Manure smells bad."), the individual can be aware of his own perceptions at the moment of perceiving, and without regard to the usual categories ("*This* grass is purple." "Going to church *this time* is harmful." "*This* manure has a rather pleasant odor."). The individual who is open to experience resists the temptation to establish rigid categories; he tolerates and even delights in ambiguity, and he is able to receive and retain conflicting information without forcing premature resolution on a situation. The individual who is open to experience realizes that reality is not a series of easily defined givens, but rather a flow of events which are unique, amorphous, and ambiguous.

The second condition for the fostering of creativity is *an internal locus of evaluation.* This is perhaps the most fundamental condition for fostering creativity. For the creative individual, the value of his product is not determined by the praise or criticism of outside agents, but by himself: My product is satisfying to *me.* It fills my basic needs for self-respect, for self-expression, for joy. If I am forced to consider the probable praise or criticism of others at each step along the way, then part of my vital energy is diverted from my creation into attempts to evaluate what it is that others would wish for. This is not to say that the creative person should be oblivious to the judgments of others. Such feedback is an important part of shaping the person's concepts of himself and of his society. But the primary locus of evaluation must remain within the creator.

The third condition is *the ability to play*, to toy with the world. This implies an ability to live for the moment without regard for future consequences. Living for the moment enhances the ability to be open to new experience, to go off on a wild goose chase, to follow a hunch. Playing also implies the ability to toss and juggle, to shape elements and ideas into wild juxtapositions and improbable hypotheses. This spontaneous toying gives rise to new combinations and surprises. It allows for the possibility of seeing life in new and significant ways. It is from this rich jumble of chaos that the new spark of creativity often jumps.

How can we imbue the classroom with these conditions that foster creativity? What can we do to allow for spontaneous play and internal evaluation? How can we build delight in the ambiguous, the different, and the unknown? The answer is not in merely letting everyone do his own thing. The answer lies with the teacher: the teacher who takes delight in novelty, in ambiguity, in absurdity; the teacher who fosters an atmosphere of joy and play and helps supply the materials, words, colors, music, costumes; the teacher who steadfastly refuses to evaluate the creative output of the student, and who helps the student to be strong enough to rely on his own internal evaluation. In the classroom of such a teacher, creativity flourishes.

HUMAN VALUES AND MORAL JUDGMENT

The classroom which fosters personal and social growth through the development of skills in human values — such as creativity, self-reliance, cooperation, and love — also encourages moral growth. For developing skill in moral judgment, as with other human survival skills, depends upon practice — upon opportunities to make and evaluate moral judgments.

The traditional means of teaching for moral development has been to drill in a set of fixed virtues, such as honesty, helpfulness, willingness to obey, etc. The teacher displays the virtue by precept and example and moral tales, and then rewards those students who conform to the virtue and punishes those who do not. This time-honored method has been noticeably unsuccessful.

Recently, however, a newer conception of moral-judgment training has begun to emerge, championed at the outset by John Dewey and Jean Piaget, and more recently by Lawrence Kohlberg. These men have assumed that the formation of moral judgment is a process of development through stages of knowing — that is, a growing awareness of the external world.

If we agree with Dewey, Piaget, and Kohlberg that the development of moral judgment is a cognitive process, rather than the absorption of an imposed set of standards, then as teachers our obligation is clear. Instead of preaching to our students about the importance of honesty, responsibility, helpfulness, and such, it is the job of teachers to set up learning experiences which will facilitate moral development.

These experiences fall under the general category of what Kohlberg calls role taking: that is, opportunities to take a variety of socially useful roles so that the student will be able to see a moral decision from a number of different perspectives. The wider the range of role experiences, the more likely the student is to make a moral decision that will be just and satisfactory to many people instead of only to himself. The critical factor in role taking is empathy. The more an individual is able to empathize with others, the more likely he is to make a just moral decision.

How can we create learning opportunities that foster role taking, that develop the power of empathy? By creating situations where students can be given both responsibility and a share in decision making at appropriate levels, and where they can see their own importance to the society in which they live.

The climate in some classrooms is naturally better adapted to provide role-taking opportunities than that in others. The classroom where students serve as student and teacher, as cook, cookie server, blackboard washer, builder of airplanes, and planner of activities is likely to promote role taking. The classroom where students are encouraged to respond only to the teacher, and are forced to await their turn for a drink of water sitting quietly with their hands folded on their desks, is not.

Role playing, a sort of simulated role-taking, is another way to promote empathy. When young children dress up as "mother" and "father" and engage in fanciful play, they are beginning to play the role of another person, beginning to build their power of empathy. The elementary school classroom which has a costume box and plenty of opportunities for children to engage in this informal role playing is naturally encouraging moral development..

Older students can be asked to role play the new boy in class, the highway builder and the farmer, Lieutenant Calley at My Lai, and a long list of real or hypothetical roles in which moral decisions must be made. Through placing themselves in a role and experiencing the processes of deciding, students can begin to see moral deciding in a larger framework than their single point of view.

Ultimately, all formal education should be moral education. The school should be a place where the activity of each individual can also be social in character — where the student can develop as an individual and at the same time use his powers to further the larger activities of the group. He should be given opportunities to play many socially useful roles through which he can both expand his awareness of his world and increase his power of empathy. It is the moral responsibility of the teacher to supply every possible aid to this process.

SOCIAL ENTROPY AND THE CURRICULUM

In providing opportunities in the curriculum for creativity and for such activities as role taking and role playing, we must examine the overall structure and content of the curriculum, and re-evaluate it in relation to our goals.

For a curriculum is very susceptible to entropy — the natural tendency of systems to break down, lose their special purposes, become undifferentiated, and fall into sameness and chaos. To illustrate this point, allow us to tell you about the time we developed a system of putting special and important telephone numbers on the outside back cover of the phone book. First to be listed was the pizza parlor so that we could quickly order up our Monday night special. Then came our doctor's number. Then the numbers of two babysitters. An emergency showed the importance of including the plumber's number there. A friend who had recently moved called from Oshkosh, and we added his number along with a few doodles. And so on. You can see, of course, what's happening. Today, the back cover is practically useless. And we've begun a new system: when either of us find one of our important numbers, like the pizza parlor, we circle it in red so that we will be able to find it easily.

The curriculum is very much like that. As more and more important things are identified for inclusion, it gets harder and harder to sort out what is important. Because we have reached the point of teaching everything all the time, we are in reality teaching nothing. Of course, reading is very important, and so we teach it. And so is algebra, and composition, and the semi-colon, and Shakespeare, and the Civil War — and now Sex Education and Drug Abuse Education.

To prevent curricular entropy, what we need is a clear notion of the difference between means values and end values. For instance, we value writing as a means of communicating with others. We value church as a means of religious expression, fire as a means of cooking our food and warming our family. For us, writing, church, and fire are means values. If other and better ways are found to accomplish the ends that they serve, then we can do without them. When they no longer serve us, we should — in fact must — do without them.

An example of entropic drift in the curriculum is the

study of Latin. Latin is useful in developing English vocabulary (means value). But if the development of a good vocabulary is an end value, then we should take a look at the other possible means of developing vocabulary — studying word lists, extensive reading, conversation, or watching television. Literature is a means of exploring and understanding the human condition. It may even be the best means. Certainly "the classics" have much to offer in the way of vicarious experience. But when this is translated into the notion that everyone *should* read *Hamlet* or *War and Peace,* then we are fueling the forces of entropy.

The problem with means values is that as they serve us, they dress themselves in the clothes of end values, becoming ends in themselves. Witness the familiar "Go to church this Sunday" type of public-service advertising, extolling the virtues of churchgoing rather than those of religious expression. "Support the College of Your Choice" and "Stay in School" campaigns have a similar nature — an unconscious shifting of means values (What is college for? What is a high school diploma for?) so that they become ends in themselves, even though they may no longer serve a beneficial social function. (Recent research indicates, for instance, that staying in high school may do more harm to some young people than dropping out.)

The people responsible for setting up and maintaining educational programs need to ask themselves again and again, "How does this serve us, how does this serve society?" We must test each value, each element of the curriculum, each institution. Moreover, we must train our young to discern means values and end values, we must equip them to see the new realities in a changing world, rather than relying on older, perhaps invalid perceptions.

The distinguishing mark of the creative person is that he can see old problems in new ways. This means accepting, encouraging, and delighting in the new, the different, the unusual. We must educate our young people to think creatively. We must educate them not to see the world as a series of givens, of single right answers, of pre-ordained limitations. We must educate them to survive by teaching them survival skills — by teaching them how to live by human values.

Means Values, End Values, and the Entropic Drift Toward False End Values

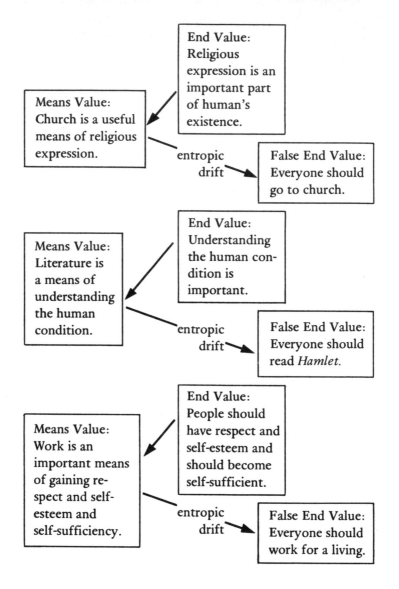

Notes

1.   Regrettably, the English language does not offer an impersonal pronoun without gender, except for the frequently inappropriate "one." To fill this void, feminists in recent years have advocated the use of "he/she," "s/he," and other somewhat awkward locutions. In this book, we use the traditional "he" as an impersonal pronoun of least stylistic difficulty. Our decision represents a choice of the least of several evils, and does not imply any statement of male supremacy or similar nonsense.

2.   *Motivation and Personality,* 2nd ed. (New York, Harper & Row, 1970).

3.   The Black Panther Party's program of giving children breakfast at school is a striking example of a plan designed with an understanding of the basic needs. Hungry children are unable to pay attention to the business of learning because their basic need for nourishment has not been filled. Filling that need has provided at least part of the answer to better education for ghetto children.

4.   "Towards a Theory of Creativity," in *A Source Book of Creative Thinking,* Sidney J. Parnes and Harold F. Harding, eds. (New York, Charles Scribner's Sons, 1962).

Part II
A Sequence of Teaching Concerns

Chapter Two

WHERE TO BEGIN

The longest journey begins with a single step.

CHINESE PROVERB

This section of the book sets forth a sequence of seven teaching concerns and related activities to help in the teaching of human values. Most sequential approaches to education deal with content: a chronological sequence in history, a sequence of operations in mathematics, a sequence from lower to higher orders in biology, and so on. The sequence of teaching concerns, on the other hand, deals with the process of learning: it is relevant for the teacher in planning any lesson, unit, or course. The seven teaching concerns are:

1. *Orientation:* Why have we all gathered here?

2. *Community Building:* How can we get to know each other better so that we can work together better?

3. *Achievement Motivation:* What are our

goals? Procedures for reaching those goals? Conditions under which to work toward those goals? What risks are we willing to take in order to attain those goals?

4. *Fostering Open Communication:* How can we communicate more openly with each other? How can we understand each other better?

5. *Information Seeking, Gathering, and Sharing:* What do we know and what do we want to know? Where can we find the information we need? What information can we share with each other?

6. *Value Exploration and Clarification:* What do we value? What life choices can we make which will reflect our values? Do we have the information we need on which to form value judgments? What additional information is needed? (See No. 5 above.)

7. *Planning for Change:* How do we want to change? What alternative courses of action are open to us? What resources are available? How can we decide which alternatives and which resources to use? How can we act on our decisions?

TRADITIONAL SCHOOLS, TRADITIONAL STUDENTS

Like all educational enterprises, the sequence of teaching

concerns is most effective when all the students in a class voluntarily pursue common ends: the most effective teaching of electricity, for example, would occur in an elective course clearly labeled "All About Electricity." Unfortunately, few schools have any system of elective courses built into their framework of compulsory attendance. Generally, a teacher and a collection of students of diverse needs and interests are stuck together for a term or a year and expected to study English, or science, or fifth grade, or whatever.

Even within this framework, the goals and perceptions of some students will be so divergent from those of the class as a whole that provision should be made for individual or small-group independent study wherever possible. Perhaps the most difficult problem in setting up this kind of departure from the traditional classroom will be with the student who perceives himself as the passive receptor for the knowledge that the teacher dispenses. Paradoxically, this "traditional" student may also be the most troublesome behavior problem when the teacher lectures or resorts to authoritarian measures.

The attitude of the traditional student is the sign of the beginnings of an authoritarian personality, one who depends upon a hierarchical decision-making structure. Unconsciously, the student attempts to move the responsibility for learning from himself to the teacher, an attempt that the teacher should steadfastly combat. While the teacher has the responsibility of helping the student learn, and of structuring situations where learning can occur, the responsibility for learning must lie with the student.

However, the teacher must recognize the legitimacy of the traditional student's concerns. For example, he might set up an independent study project that would reflect traditional goals. Say that the student expects to study grammar: the teacher might set up a project where he can do so independently and then be tested on his achievement by some standard test. Then, gradually, as the student learns the art of learning, the teacher can help him to take a larger part in setting his own goals for his learning.

THE NEW TEACHER

Using the sequence of teaching concerns presented here implies a new and different role for the teacher: he is not merely a dispenser of knowledge. Although he may have expert knowledge in a certain field — and it is proper for him to share this knowledge with his students, even in the form of a lecture — he cannot be expected to possess all the information that his students may want and need. Instead, he is a helper — helping students to diagnose their wants and their needs, helping them to identify information and material resources, helping them to set up useful learning situations, and helping them to develop skills in creative and critical thinking. It is vital for this new kind of teacher to possess knowledge not so much of his subject matter, but of how people learn and how he can help them learn.

THE INTERACTION OF TEACHING CONCERNS

The seven teaching concerns are not mutually exclusive, but frequently overlap or reinforce each other. Orientation, for instance, has a lot to do with achievement motivation, and achievement motivation is a form of value exploration in itself. Developing a sense of community involves increasing effectiveness in communication skills, and vice-versa.

For instance, if electricity is the subject of a unit, the teacher might start by asking the class to "brainstorm" — shoot out ideas at random for three or four minutes — everything they know about electricity. (For more about brainstorming, see page 38). The teacher records these items on the board. This is a kind of orientation or introduction to the unit. It also serves as a community-building activity, since the "rules" of brainstorming (see page 38) emphasize acceptance and respect for the contributions of all.

After the brainstorming session, the teacher may ask the students to spend two minutes thinking about and writing down on paper what things they want to know about electricity. These questions are written on the blackboard, and now the business of goal-setting, or achievement motivation, has begun. Information seeking, gathering, and sharing has also been going on right from the start, and it continues as students attempt to answer each other's questions.

Then the teacher may ask the students to look at the board and select the three questions that are most interesting or most important to them; this is a form of value exploration and clarification. The students may form task groups with others who are interested in exploring the same questions. They identify resources for information, and proceed to the task of gaining more information on the questions of interest to them. These task groups can later share the results of their study with the class through group reports or displays.

BRAINSTORMING AS A WAY OF THINKING

Brainstorming is perhaps the most important single skill in the entire repertory of personal-growth activities. The conscientious use of brainstorming and adherence to its rules produces a versatile, creative, mind-expanding way of thinking. The rules should be reviewed often, and it is probably a good idea to discuss the rationale for each with the class.

Rules of Brainstorming

1. Express no negative evaluation of any idea presented.

2. Work for quantity, not quality — the longer the list of ideas, the better.

3. Expand on each other's ideas, piggyback — if someone's idea prompts an idea in your head, then share it with the class.

4. Encourage zany, far-out ideas.

5. Record each idea, at least by a key word or phrase.

6. Set a time limit for the brainstorming session and hold strictly to it.

Brainstorming helps to generate a large volume of ideas. It encourages germs of ideas, half-formed ideas; it gives good ideas with some drawbacks a chance to grow and develop. And it turns group problem-solving away from a competitive, one-upping atmosphere toward a truly collaborative venture, where the main adversary is the problem to be solved rather than others in the group.

In a larger sense, the rules of brainstorming form the structure for the human-values classroom as a place where all are accepted for what they are, where all may try without fear of failure, where active collaboration is encouraged, and where creativity, individuality, unorthodoxy are respected.

Briefly, here is a rationale for the rules of brainstorming:

1. *Express no negative evaluation:* A ban on negativity encourages participants to speak freely without worrying whether their ideas are good enough to be shared. It says, "All ideas welcomed here."

2. *Work for quantity:* This rule helps the flow of ideas by adding a game-like tension to the activity. Quality is a by-product of quantity. The longer the list, the more likely it is to contain a number of workable ideas. This rule encourages everyone to try without the jeopardy of failure.

3. *Expand on each other's ideas:* This rule suggests to students that they can help each other. When one person elaborates on another's idea, he is paying a compliment to that person, accepting him, appreciating his contribution, showing him to be a worthy collaborator. This rule can help change the classroom from a battleground with winners and losers to a place where all can win.

4. *Encourage zany, far-out ideas:*   Many weird ideas have a useful kernel which may not be evident to the proponent of the idea but which is picked up later by the group. And a zany idea may trigger a useful idea in someone else's mind. Problems are often seen in new ways as a result of this practice.

5. *Record each idea:*   This rule reinforces the acceptance of each idea and provides for a mechanism for deferring evaluation. These brainstorm lists can be thought of as rich deposits which can be later mined and shaped to meet specific needs.

6. *Set a time limit:*   This rule takes away the pressure for perfection. Time is seen as a valuable resource to be taken into account in any undertaking. Generally, where a time limit is established and adhered to, personal commitment is high, because individuals are relieved of the tension of determining when they have worked long enough to satisfy the requirements of the task.

PRACTICING BRAINSTORMING

Brainstorming is a skill which can be improved through practice. The rules should be reviewed before each brainstorming session and posted on the blackboard or wall. Brainstorming can be done by the entire class or in small groups. (Groups of five or six are small enough so that no one need wait to offer his idea, yet large enough so that the variety of ideas is stimulating.)

When the entire class brainstorms, it may be necessary to have two or three recorders at the blackboards so that they can keep up with the fast-flowing ideas. (Brainstorming is no time for raised hands or other such formalities.) When small groups brainstorm, it is important to cross-fertilize by having the recorder for each group read the group's list to the entire class. Where time is a problem, groups can pair and read their lists to each other. Another way of sharing group lists is to have each person in the group pick the idea he likes the most from the group's list, and then have this select list read to the entire class.

"Warm-Up Brainstorms" should be on playful subjects to encourage and show acceptance of zany, far-out ideas. Here are some possible topics for Warm-Up Brainstorms:

1. You have been stranded on an uninhabited tropical island. Food and water are no problem. You have only one artifact of civilization — an empty Coke bottle. Brainstorm uses for the Coke bottle. *(Time limit: five minutes.)*

2. Brainstorm ways to improve on the common bathtub. *(Time limit: five minutes.)*

3. Brainstorm uses for a fire hydrant (junk automobiles, broken baseball bats, tabs from flip-top cans, old wheel covers). *(Time limit: five minutes.)*

4. Brainstorm ways to send love to someone far

away.   *(Time limit: seven minutes.)*

5.   Brainstorm new kitchen appliances. *(Time limit: seven minutes.)*

6.   Brainstorm zany topics for further Warm-Up Brainstorms.   *(Time limit: five minutes.)*

Brainstorming is a good method for finding solutions to problems. An individual can bring a problem to a small group, such as, "How can I get along better with my brother?" He spends one or two minutes filling in the group on the background of the problem. The group then brainstorms solutions to his problem for a specific amount of time (usually no longer than ten minutes). The individual whose problem it is acts as recorder. He can then select the most promising solutions and write a self-contract (see page 44).

The class as a whole might brainstorm problems that young people their age might have. One problem from the brainstorming list is selected for an alternative search by the whole class, or the class may divide into groups, with each group choosing a problem from the list.

Sample alternative search questions:

1.   Ways to spend spring vacation.

2.   Ways to make Thanksgiving more meaningful.

3.   Ways to increase your circle of friends.

4.   What to do if your good friend offers you LSD.

5.   Ways to save money.

Often, self-contracting is a useful follow-up to an alternative search brainstorm. Once a person has selected a course of action which may lead toward the solution or reduction of a problem, he can write a contract (see page 44) with himself specifying what he is going to do, how long he will keep at it, and what observable indications of success he will use to evaluate his action. Since research indicates that about three weeks are necessary for a new pattern of behavior to become fully functional, the final evaluation of the self-contract should come about three weeks after the initiation of the contract.

A self-contract is personal and private. The teacher or other members of the class should never ask to see it. If the student wants to show it to the teacher or others, that, of course, is permissible.

Personal Self-Contract Form

_____

DATE

Contract period: _____

Statement of the problem: _____

_____

Actions to be taken: _____

_____

Observable behaviors to indicate success: _____

_____

End-of-first-week review (comment): _____

_____

End-of-second-week review (comment): _____

_____

Final (end-of-third-week) review (comment): _____

_____

Provisions for a new contract: _____

_____

Chapter Three

ORIENTATION

Any time people get together, one of the first considerations is orientation — creating a mind set that is conducive to open communication. We tend to do this naturally in informal situations: the small talk that often takes place at the beginning of a business meeting, for instance, gets the participants used to hearing each other's voices and gives them some common ground. The opening few lines of a play or the initial bars of a symphony prepare the listener for what is to follow and introduce him to the general theme or tone of the piece. The illustrations or action behind the opening credits of a movie or television show have much the same purpose. Even this paragraph is intended to orient the reader to the content of this section.

FIRST THINGS

At the beginning of a new school year or term, particularly when the students and the teacher don't know one another and/or are unfamiliar with their immediate environment (such as seventh graders entering a large regionalized junior high school), there are a few items of information which must take top priority in order to eliminate unnecessary tensions. The list includes the teacher's name and how he or she wishes to be addressed (e.g. Miss, Mrs., or Ms.), the name and section number of the class (with time allowed for lost souls to get directions and leave), when the period ends, where the nearest bathrooms are, where students may put extra books and gear in order not to clutter the floor — the simple, straightforward information which helps students to gain a sense of security in what otherwise might seem a hostile environment.

The student whose attention is absorbed by the problem of finding a bathroom before his next class is not able to contribute to or benefit from what is going on in the classroom. Like the hungry child, his psychic energy is being consumed by trying to satisfy a more basic need.

By giving his students the information they need in order to feel somewhat secure in their situation, to have a sense of control over their own lives, the teacher frees their minds for the common task at hand.

INTRODUCING THE LESSON

In teaching, introducing the lesson, or the content of the unit, or the work of the term is an important but often neglected consideration. One of the teacher's first tasks is to communicate to the students the goals of the class as the teacher sees them. Any activity that catches the students' attention and interests them in the lesson is an appropriate means of orientation.

For instance, to begin a lesson on oxidation, a science teacher can light a candle, watch it burn for a few moments, place it under a bell jar, watch it go out, and then ask: "What made the flame go out?" A social studies teacher can ask which of his students are Roman Catholic, assign them to the back seats in the classroom, and thus begin a unit on religious persecution. Or an English teacher can ask the class to brainstorm all the uses of language as an introduction to a unit on that subject.

Analogies or demonstrations or intriguing problems are all possible ways to introduce a lesson or unit. Variety is important — the chemistry teacher who starts every class with some kind of explosion, for instance, may find that the students soon become blasé about his opening blasts. But more important than variety is relevance. The most effective introductions build on the students' present knowledge and skills to interest them in learning more. The English teacher who asks the students to brainstorm the uses of language is getting a picture of the present level of knowledge, and he will be able to refer to the brainstormed list throughout the term in planning future lessons. As students in the social studies class discuss their emotional reactions to the segregation of Roman Catholic students, they grow cognitively in their awareness of religious persecution.

In other words, the teacher must diagnose the students' needs and evaluate how best to make use of their present level of knowledge.

FOCUSING THE SUBJECT

Another consideration in orientation is focusing: does the introduction focus the subject clearly enough for the class to deal with it significantly? The science teacher has focused clearly on the process of oxidation rather than on the uses or the by-products of burning. The English teacher, on the other hand, may need to refine his focus within the broad area of the uses of language. He might do this by asking his students to pick the three uses of language that they consider most interesting or most important. This would have the additional advantage of letting the students help in choosing aspects of the subject that interest them most. Or the teacher might combine the focus that the students have selected with the concerns that he, from his own experience and knowledge, feels will be most valuable to his students.

ESTABLISHING RULES AND PROCEDURES

Nothing is more enervating than the chaos and confusion that go with lack of discipline or unclear priorities. In creating learning opportunities and helping students to use those learning opportunities, the teacher inevitably finds himself responsible for establishing order, discipline, and priorities. But this responsibility does not imply an arbitrary or autocratic rule. The teacher's role is to help with the establishment of a hierarchy of needs and of mutually acceptable ground rules for meeting those needs.

Since the needs and expectations of each group of students are to some extent unique, as are those of each teacher, the teacher must be responsive to the needs and expectations of the class and explicit about his own expectations. In establishing rules and procedures, it is important for the teacher to reaffirm the fact that he is not abdicating his responsibility to the students. The teacher's responsibility to his students and the students' responsibility to each other should undergo continual definition through the term or year.

One good way to get students involved in establishing rules and procedures is for the class to meet as a whole, with chairs or desks moved into a tight circle (chairs alone if possible). The teacher should sit as a member of the circle and not in a position traditionally associated with power, such as in front of the blackboard or behind the big desk. The teacher or one of the students may moderate. The objective is to reach consensus on priorities, rules, and other matters that may arise. The teacher should point out any rules that he thinks may be unworkable or that might pit him against the class as the enforcer.

Another good method is for the class to divide into groups of four or five to discuss and make recommendations about rules, procedures, problems. It is important that the task be concrete and clearly understood, and that a definite time limit be placed upon the discussions. All groups can work on the same task, or the tasks can be divided among the groups. After these discussions, the class meets as a whole to discuss and act upon the recommendations of the small groups.

Or, the teacher may prefer to set up a task force on rules and procedures: a six-member group with staggered membership, so that each week one member is replaced. The newly appointed members will each serve a six-week term until all students have served. This task force can operate during class time while other groups are engaged in other activities, and can report to the class weekly.

Chapter Four

COMMUNITY BUILDING

Building a sense of community in the classroom is vital both to the narrow goals of the classroom and to the broader goals of education. Community building is, in fact, a survival skill. One of the clearest messages of the post-World War II era, with its atomic threat, ecology crisis, and population explosion, is that if we fail to develop a world community, we will not have a world. Therefore, the greatest goal of the school may well be to foster in young persons a responsiveness to the needs of other people and other groups, starting with the microcosm of the classroom. Only by encouraging attitudes of concern and unconditional positive regard for others can we counteract the destructive norms of self-interest that prevail in our society today.

As to academic goals, a great deal of evidence suggests that academic achievement is likely to increase when a high level of rapport exists among the students and between students and teacher, and when influence and friendship are not the prerogatives of just a few members of the class. In a classroom community, the attitudes of the students toward the academic goals of the class are more positive, students derive more satisfaction from pursuing the goals of the class, and they learn more.

Building community helps to fill basic human needs at many levels — security, belongingness, love, respect, self-esteem. When there is little feeling of community in a classroom, students are likely to feel anxiety, hostility, self-doubt, rejection. And all these negative feelings are likely to contribute to unconstructive behavior — behavior which, paradoxically, is likely to be self-perpetuating, as teacher disapproval leads to more feelings of rejection, which in turn triggers unconstructive behavior, which again . . .

Peer influence and support is also important in helping the young person move from dependency upon adults towards self-sufficiency. Where the importance of community and positive peer relations is understood, there is more chance for an easy transition to maturity, instead of one that is cataclysmic and destructive.

CHARACTERISTICS OF COMMUNITY

Building community in the classroom takes time and commitment. It is an ongoing process that must continue throughout the life of the class. Here are some of the characteristics that a teacher can work for in creating community.

1. Students share influence with each other and with the teacher.

2. There is a high level of rapport in the class as a

whole and among individual students.

3. The attitudes of the students support the goals of the class.

4. The attitudes of the students support and encourage individual differences among their peers.

5. There is open and honest communication both among the students and between the students and the teacher.

6. There is a feeling of shared responsibility among the students and with the teacher to maintain and improve the community, and to further the goals of the class.[1]

In building community, the teacher must be quite explicit about the importance of community, for many students may regard it as a waste of time. It may be useful for the teacher to conduct periodic or continuing discussions on "Where are we as a group?" For best results, the teacher should encourage students to take responsibility for building and maintaining a sense of community in the classroom.

PROBLEMS IN COMMUNITY BUILDING

Specific problems in building or maintaining the community may require special measures. For instance, where one or several students are rejected by others, role playing may be useful to help develop empathy and understanding. The teacher might place an open chair at the front of the room, give the chair a fictitious name, and then ask the members of the class to think of the things that the fictitious person could do that would "turn people off." As the students contribute, the teacher notes each item on the board. Then a second chair is placed at the front and the process is repeated, this time with "things that would make others like you."

Now these two chairs engage in an imaginary meeting. The teacher sets up the situation: "Suppose these two people met in the hall. Who would start the conversation, and what would he say?" When someone contributes the opening line, then the teacher says, "And how would the other respond?" The open-chair role play is continued for two or three minutes. Afterward, the class discusses what went on and how the two might gain a better understanding of each other.

Using the open chairs instead of actual students gives a certain amount of protection to individuals who may wish to post problems or state points of view but who do not have sufficient ego strength to role play in front of a class. After the initial "open chair" session, some students may be willing and eager to sit in the chairs and play the roles. This is often a productive extension of the activity.

Another common problem in classroom community occurs at the beginning of a term or year when several new students join the class. The teacher might ask the "veterans" of the class to think of instances when they came into a group for the first time. Next, the teacher asks for volunteers who will recount their experiences and tell how it felt to be new in a group. Then the teacher asks the students to each write down three or four questions that they might ask in order to get to know somebody. Each of the students may then go to a person whom they don't know well or at all, and spend four minutes getting better acquainted by posing some of their questions. At the end of the four minutes, the teacher asks the pairs to spend two more minutes working together trying to identify things that they have in common.

At this point, the teacher has many options, such as: (1) He could ask the students to leave their partners, find new partners, and repeat the process. (2) He could ask pairs to join into groups of four, with each person introducing his partner to the other members of the group. (3) He could conduct a general discussion focusing on things that the students may have in common. They could touch on the feelings that people have in new situations, and discuss how the class can become a better community.

A FEW WORDS ABOUT ACTIVITIES

Before moving on to community-building activities, let us say first that almost all the activities in this book are community-building in nature. Those presented below are specifically designed to build community and to provide practice in interpersonal relationships.

We have not suggested time allotments for most of the activities presented because classes vary in their needs for discussion and explanation. Generally, each activity in this book can be completed within a forty-five minute period. However, activities often take longer than expected, and it is important to allow sufficient time for small group and class discussion and for reflection, so that the data elicited can be evaluated and assimilated. Teachers new to personal-growth activities almost always go too fast rather than too slow.

The activities have been designed with a class of twenty to thirty students in mind, but they have been used in classes of anywhere from twelve to thirty-five students. There is considerable room for flexibility in breaking up the large group into smaller units of various sizes for activities.

Teachers should be warned against expecting an activity to produce immediately observable behavioral changes. Personal growth is a life-long process, and personal-growth activities often produce significant behavior changes months or even years after the activity has occurred.

Lastly, critics of personal growth activities often complain that the activities are gimmicks, or are "contrived." Fritz Perls, the founder of Gestalt therapy, has pointed out that a gimmick is what a person calls a technique when he doesn't understand it. Sonnets and football games are contrived, and so are the College Board exams.

THE RIGHT TO PASS

In all personal growth activities, the right of any individual to pass—to withhold his thoughts and ideas, to refrain from participating—must be respected and reinforced with dignity. The teacher, as group facilitator, is in a key position to foster the attitude that a pass represents a conscious act by an individual which must be respected by all.

The motives for passing are so varied and often so complex that group members should refrain from conjecture as to why an individual is passing. For instance, the passer might find the topic too deeply personal to share his thoughts; or the topic might touch off inchoate memories which tie his tongue; or he might feel that his thoughts are irrelevant, or might be taken as misleading, or have been expressed so often as to become trite. He might feel that he is protecting someone else or himself. Or he might be concentrating on the group process as an observer and be unwilling or unable to shift his focus. And, of course, he might be thinking of something entirely off the subject or even be day-dreaming. It is crucial for the teacher to establish the sanctity of the pass early in the program.

ACTIVITIES FOR COMMUNITY BUILDING

Subject: *Name Tags.*

Material: File cards, masking tape, magic markers, pencils or pens.

Procedure:

1. Select three or four volunteers and equip each with a magic marker and a stack of file cards. Each student goes to one of the volunteers and tells the volunteer the name that he wishes to be called in the class. The volunteer writes that name in large letters on the file card and gives it to the student.

2. When all the students have received name tags, the

teacher tells them that name tags are a good way to get to know each other and that they can carry other information besides the name. The teacher asks each student to write in the upper right-hand corner of his name tag one place that he would like to live for a year (not his present home). In the upper left-hand corner, one thing that he has in his home that he is proud of. In the lower right-hand corner, one famous living person whom he would like to resemble in some way. In the lower left-hand corner, one thing that he is good at doing. Then the tape is passed around and each person tapes his name tag on in a conspicuous place.

3. The teacher may then divide the class into groups of four or five and ask each member to spend one minute telling his group about the words on his name tag. Or, the teacher may proceed with some other activity and simply suggest that the students use the name tags as the basis for informal conversations during a lull. The teacher should be sure to wear a name tag bearing the same information, and be prepared to share the information with his students if that seems to be appropriate.

4. At the end of the class, the teacher may either collect the name tags or ask that the student save the tags for class the next day. Some teachers ask that name tags be worn each day for the first week of class. Extra name tag materials should be available at no penalty for those who fail to bring their name tags to class. Each day, during the name-tag-wearing period, the teacher may ask the students to freshen up the name tag by putting some new information on it.

5. Here are some other things that can be used for name tag information: the name of a historical figure that you would like to resemble; three things that you love to do; five things that describe you ending in -*able*; five things that you value ending in *ing*; your nominee for President of the United States; three jobs that you think you would like to try for a year.

NOTE: Not all of this information need be shared fully for this exercise to be valuable; the reflective thinking involved has value in itself. Some students may object to wearing name tags for a whole week, and just as in any other personal-growth activity, their right to pass should be honored. This is a positive focus activity; avoid using items that might have negative connotations (three things in my house I'd like to get rid of).

Subject: *Address List.*

Material: Clipboard, purple ditto master, pencil.

Procedure:

1. Publish a list of the names and addresses of all the students in the class with telephone numbers and birthdays. Pass around a purple ditto master on a clipboard with lines and spaces for each person: name, address, telephone number, and birthday.

2. Run off the list and distribute it the next day. The

implication here is that members of this class will want to communicate with each other outside of school. This is a bridge between the artificial world of the classroom and the real world outside.

Subject: *Singing Sam.*

Material: None.

Procedure:

1. This is a mnemonic device for getting students to learn each other's names quickly. The class is seated in a circle. Teacher or first student leads off with, "I'm (Singing) (Sam)," filling in the first blank with something he's good at and the second blank with the name he wishes to be called in this class. The second person says, "He's Singing Sam, and I'm (Knitting) (Barbara)," filling in the blanks as before.

2. This name reciting proceeds around the circle, adding the name of each person in order and ending when the first person repeats the names and good-at's for each person in the group.

NOTE: This is not a contest but just a way to get to know names quickly. There should be no penalty for not being able to recite all the names, but when someone is stuck, the teacher might say, "Can someone help him?" This is a positive focus activity.

Subject: *Magic Box.*

Material: 3 x 5 file cards, pencils or pens.

Procedure:

1. Students are seated in groups of five or six. Teacher tells the students to imagine that while they have been in school this day, a box has been delivered to each student's home. It is a magic box of any dimensions the student wants, and it contains any one thing that the student would want. Each student writes his wish on a 3 x 5 card.

2. One person collects all the cards, shuffles them, and reads them one at a time while all try to guess the authors.

IMPORTANT NOTE: Here and in any other activity which involves the sharing of personal desires, feelings, hopes, etc., it is extremely important that the teacher announce the procedure for the entire activity at the beginning, *so that the students know in advance that they will be asked to share what they write.* It is impossible to overstress the importance of doing this. If, in the students' eyes, the teacher fails to communicate fully and openly, whether intentionally or not, he risks destroying whatever positive relationship has developed between himself and the class.

3. As an extension of this activity, the teacher might ask each group to spend ten minutes deciding on one item

for the group's magic box. This must be an item which does *not* appear on the list of items for individuals in the group.

4. The students might be asked to reflect for a few moments as to whether they would be willing to trade their individual items for the group item. Voluntary comments can be called for.

Subject: *Paper Profiles.*

Material: Construction paper, newspaper, magic markers, scissors, glue, light source, *Profile Questionnaires* (see page 63).

Procedure:

1. Each student is asked to pick a page of newspaper which is in some way representative of himself. (This activity is facilitated by asking students to bring in the page from home, but the teacher should have extra newspaper for those who for one reason or another do not bring in newspaper. There should be no penalty for students failing to supply materials for these activities.)

2. Students work in groups of three. In turn each student's newspaper is taped to the wall; the student sits with the side of his head facing the newspaper, about three inches away from it. The light source is placed about six inches

away from the student's head. One of the other two students in the group traces the outline of the shadow, thus providing a profile on the newspaper.

3. Each student cuts out his own profile and mounts it on construction paper. Then each student fills out his own *Profile Questionnaire,* consulting with the others in his group for advice and comment if he wishes. (The filling out of questionnaires can go on while waiting for a turn at the light source.)

4. The *Profile Questionnaire* is taped under the finished profile and all the profiles are displayed on the wall for about a week. At the end of the display period, the profiles are taken down and saved so they can be posted again on the last day of class.

Subject: *Color Profiles.*

Procedure: Same as "Paper Profiles," except that each student chooses a piece of colored construction paper for his profile instead of the newspaper.

Profile Questionnaire

Name _____

I like to be called _____

Address _____
_____

Phone number _____

Birthday _____

Hobbies _____
_____

Favorite record _____

Favorite TV show _____

Favorite sports_____

Favorite movie, TV, or sports stars _____
_____

Favorite character from a book _____

What I'd like to be doing in ten years_____
_____
_____

Quote, comment, thought for the day, or favorite saying:
_____
_____
_____
_____

Subject: *Photo Profiles.*

Material: Polaroid or other simple camera (preferably with flash), scissors, construction paper, glue, *Profile Questionnaires* (see page 63).

Procedure:

1. Students take Polaroid snapshots of each other, or the class camera buff takes pictures of each member of the class.

2. The pictures are mounted on construction paper and the *Profile Questionnaire* is attached below.

Subject: *Self-Collage.*

Material: Old magazines, newspapers, 8½ x 11 inch construction paper, glue, scissors, tape, 3 x 5 cards.

Time: This activity will require two 40-minute periods.

Procedure:

1. Each student is asked to select one or two magazines or newspapers and one piece of colored construction paper. With these materials, the student is to make a collage of pictures and words that represents his *ideal* self.

2. In groups of four to six, each student displays his collage

and says whatever he would like to say about it. Then all the collages are displayed on the walls with the creator's name on a 3 x 5 card below.

3. After the collages have been displayed for a few days, they are taken down and saved. After two or three months the collages may be displayed again, this time identified by a number rather than the creator's name. Students then are asked to guess the creator of each collage.

ACTIVITIES FOR INTERPERSONAL RELATIONSHIPS

Interpersonal skills support community efforts. Indeed, interpersonal skills can be viewed as the building blocks of community, in the classroom and outside. The activities which follow help to develop such skills as: the ability to identify and build on strengths in others; giving and receiving precise positive feedback; active listening; empathizing; the ability to both give and seek direction in working toward common goals.

Subject: *Process Observer.*

Material: *Process Observer Sheets* (see page 67), pens or pencils.

Procedure:

1. For each task group in the activities on pages 70-82,

one or more persons are designated as process observers and given *Process Observer Sheets.* The process observer sits outside the group and takes no part in the task. His job is to observe the group as though it were a machine — to see how it functions, and to identify special features that help or harm its functioning.

2. When the task is completed, the task group reassembles to hear the report of the process observer. No one may interrupt him while he is reporting. After his report, there can be a general discussion of the process and the task.

NOTE: *Process Observer Sheets* can be used any time a group is involved in a task where group decisions are involved. Process observation is especially recommended for "Play Ball," "Bridge Building," "Beauty Contest," and "Tinker Toys." Not only will the process observer provide useful information to the members of the group, but also his presence serves as a reminder to group members that the objective of the exercise is to study group process. Process observation is a skill that improves with practice — don't expect "professional" process observers the very first time. Moveover, individually directed positive feedback can be helpful not only to the receiving individual but also to the entire group. Try to be as specific as possible. (E.g. "Mary, when you suggested that the group try to isolate three ideas, that seemed to break the logjam and was the beginning of the solution.") Avoid individually directed negative feedback — chances are that all members of the group are aware of individual shortcomings.

Process Observer Sheet

Directions: Your job is to observe the group as it works. Try to keep your eyes on how the group functions and what individuals *do* and *say* to help the group with its task. Resist the temptation to become involved with the task itself. Familiarize yourself with the items below so that you will have specific things to watch for. If there is more than one process observer, you may wish to divide the items among you. At the end of the task, you will be asked to report on questions below. On a separate piece of paper, list each of the group members' names, leaving a space for individually directed positive feedback.

1. What was the atmosphere in which the group worked (joyful, frivolous, tense, excited)?

2. How did the group reach decisions?

3. How did the group handle conflict (humor, sarcasm, open confrontation, shouting, withdrawing)?

4. To what extent were the members of the group involved in the task? Were there any procedures which helped get people involved?

5. How did the group treat male/female differences?

6. How did the group decide who would speak and when?

7. How well did the group members listen to each other?

8. Were there any leaders? How did they arise?

9. How did the group delegate responsibility?

Subject: *Play Ball.*[2]

Material: Rubber play balls about eight inches in diameter — one ball for each group of six to ten, *Play Ball Process Sheets* (see page 70), pencils.

Procedure:

1. The class is divided into groups of six to ten members. The teacher places a ball in the center of each group and issues the following instructions:

    "Each group is to invent a game to be played with the ball which you have been given. You will be allowed ten minutes to plan the game. At the end of that time, you should be prepared to demonstrate the game to the other members of the class. You may use any other material that is available to you. The game must be designed so that it can be played in an approved place."

(The teacher designates approved places — gym, play-ground, sidewalk, or whatever is available.)

2. At the end of ten minutes, *Play Ball Process Sheets* are handed out, and students are asked to take two or three minutes to fill them in while the planning session is still fresh in their minds.

3. Each group demonstrates its game for a five-minute period.

4. A general discussion follows, focusing on the process each group used to design its game. Students should be discouraged from thinking of the activity as a competition for the best game.

Play Ball Process Sheet

1. What part of the final plan do you feel was your contribution?

2. Did you feel free to contribute your ideas?

3. How was the leadership of the group handled? What people acted as leader(s)?

4. On a scale of one to seven, how satisfied are you with the final plan?

5. Could you have made up a better game alone?

6. Does the game take into account the varieties of abilities present in your group?

7. Does your game have provisions for rule enforcement? Why or why not?

8. To what degree was the game designed to—

   Reveal individual prowess?

emphasize collaboration among team members?

emphasize competition?

keep all participants active?

allow for creative interpretations?

9. What sort of scoring provision has your group made? How does this reflect the values of your group?

10. Open comment:

Subject: *Rushin' Baseball.*[3]

Material: Playground ball (about eight inches in diameter); baseball or softball bat, old tennis racquet, or other type of batting instrument; marker for home plate; *Rules Sheets* (see page 73).

Procedure:

1. Teacher distributes *Rules for Rushin' Baseball Sheet* and goes over them briefly, indicating that the rules will clarify themselves as the game goes on. The teacher then suggests that the class divide into two teams, letting the students determine how this is to be done. (Later, the

process of determining how to divide — and the values behind the method used — can be discussed.) The teacher also allows the students to decide which team is to bat first.

2. The game begins, with the teacher taking part (if he and the students are willing) but refusing to be cast into the role of umpire or arbiter of rules. The teacher should be very explicit about this point: if rules changes or additions are to be made, they must be made by the players themselves. (The teacher should refrain from any but the most basic clarification of the existing rules.)

3. At the end of the game, there is a general discussion focusing on issues of competition, the use of rules, the use of games (for fun, for power, for what?), what constitutes "dirty" and "clean" play, and the decision-making processes used by the members of each team and between teams. If one or two individuals would prefer to act as process observers (see page 65), their comments would be useful at this time.

NOTE: The teacher should terminate the game in time to allow at least ten minutes for a follow-up discussion. This game can be played on almost any open terrain. To adapt the game for use in a gymnasium, make home plate the jump circle in the center of the basketball court; first base can be one of the foul-shooting circles, and second base can be out the door at the other end of the gym. Players punch the ball with a closed fist instead of batting.

"Siamese Baseball" is a variation for use with large numbers of players: Members of the team at bat form pairs and must stay together, holding hands while batting and running.

Rules for Rushin' Baseball

I. *The Playing Field:*

    A.   First base is six to ten feet from home plate. It is large enough to hold ten to fifteen players at a time.

    B.   Second base is a great distance from first base and home plate. It is also large enough for most of one team.

    C.   There is no third base — go home from second.

    D.   There are no base lines: Runners may run anywhere they please (e.g. into the woods or behind the barn).

    E.   There is no "foul" territory: All hits are fair, including "foul tips."

II. *Pitching:*   The pitcher is a member of your own team. It is up to him to pitch the ball so that you can hit it. The pitcher may pitch from any location.

III. *Batting:*

    A.   Each batter bats until he hits the ball or the ball hits him (this counts as a hit ball, too, and he should run to first).

    B.   The batter is out if:
        1.   He hits a fly ball which is caught.
        2.   He fails to reach first base before the

fielded ball does.

3. He is tagged with the ball or hit by the thrown ball before he reaches first.

C. Every person on the team bats once each inning (regardless of the number of outs).

D. The pitcher is the last person to bat (someone else from his team pitches to him). Because he is the last batter, the team in the field ends the inning by getting the ball back to home plate. No runs score after this. In order for the pitcher to score, he must hit a home run.

IV. *Base Running:*

A. Any number of runners may be on a base at any time. The runners may pile up and all run together if they choose. (Therefore, there is no such thing as a force-out, except for the batter running to first.) Runners may advance on a fly ball before the ball is caught.

B. The runner may be put out when he is off the base by
   1. Being tagged with the ball.
   2. Being hit by a thrown or batted ball.

C. As soon as the ball is returned to the pitcher, all runners must stop and return to the last base they touched.

D. Runners may not leave the base until the ball is hit.

Subject: *The Leader and the Led.*

Material: Any handy building material, such as soda straws, modeling clay, computer cards, Tinker Toys, magazines and tape, papercups, pencils.

NOTE: The instructions which follow are for twenty-one participants. The teacher can adjust the numbers up or down to suit the size of the particular class.

Procedure:

1.   Divide the class into three groups of seven, designated A, B, and C. Ask each group to prepare lottery slips marked 1-7. Slips are shaken in a hat or box and then drawn, so that each person is assigned a number.

2.   Each group is asked to split into subgroups — 1, 2, and 3 together and 4, 5, 6, and 7 together. There should be six subgroups.

3.   In the middle of each subgroup place one box of soda straws, one packet of modeling clay, and one two-inch stack of used computer cards (or other building materials). Subgroup members may have one minute to examine, handle, test the properties of the building materials, at the end of which time the materials must be returned to the middle of the subgroup.

4.   The teacher then issues the following instructions: "You will have seven minutes to plan a structure to be built

from these materials; the structure is to be judged for height, stability, beauty, and use of materials. You may not touch the materials until the planning period is over. After the planning period, there will be a ten-minute building period, during which time the builders will not be allowed to talk. You may draw plans during the planning period, but you may not refer to them during the building period."

5. At the end of the planning period, teacher hands secret written instructions to the three Number One's from the original lottery. Secret instructions: for A-1 — "Role play an authoritarian leader"; for B-1 — "Role play a permissive leader"; for C-1 — "Role play the leader in a participatory democrary."

6. Teacher gives these instructions before the building period begins: "Groups A and B are to act as if they were in a dictatorship: Numbers A-4, 5, 6, and 7 and B-4, 5, 6, and 7 have become workers; numbers A-1 and B-1 have become dictators, and A-2 and 3 and B-2 and 3 are the dictator's lieutenants. During the building period, the workers may touch the materials but may not talk; the dictators may talk only to their lieutenants. The lieutenants may talk only to the workers. Dictators and lieutenants may not touch the materials. Workers will build the structure which is dictated by the dictator and his lieutenants.

7. The teacher continues: "Group C is a participatory democracy. Number One has been designated as your

leader. In this group, all may touch the materials and build, but no one, not even Number One, may talk." The teacher clarifies, answers questions, etc.

8. At the end of the ten-minute building period, the leaders are to direct their workers to judge each of the three structures. A general discussion should follow, allowing workers to speak first.

Subject: *Beauty Contest.*

Material: Old magazines, tape.

Procedure:

1. The class is divided into groups of six to eight, with at least one process observer (see page 65). Each group receives a small stack of magazines and a roll of tape.

2. The teacher instructs the students: "You are to design and build a thing of beauty. You will have eight minutes for planning and then ten minutes for building. During the planning period, you may touch the materials, but you may not pre-fabricate any parts. You may plan to acquire other material, but you may not leave your planning location until the building period begins. The magazines and tape are for your use in building if you want them. You may use any other materials which are available to you. Part of your task is to expand the

available resources as much as you need within the restrictions of time, space, and morality."

3. After the planning period and the building period, group discussions should follow, with comments from the process observers. The activity can be concluded with a general discussion focusing on: the process of group decision-making; ways to expand available resources; the significance of "beauty"; and the degree to which groups felt that they were competing with each other.

Subject: *Bridge Building.*[4]

Material: A six-inch or eight-inch stack of newspapers and a roll of masking tape for each group, *Process Observer Sheets* (see page 67), pencils, a weight such as three bricks bound together, and a cardboard box about a foot high and a foot wide.

Procedure:

1. Divide the class into groups of five to eight students with at least one process observer (see page 65). Place a stack of newspapers and a roll of masking tape in the center of each group. The bricks and cardboard box should be placed in the center of the room, equidistant from each group.

2. The teacher instructs the students: "You are to use the

newspapers and tape to design and build a bridge which will be strong enough to carry the weight of the three bricks placed on the middle of the span, and high and wide enough for the box to pass under. You may use no external supports such as a wall or chair, but you may tape your structure to the floor if you wish. You will be allowed ten minutes for planning and ten minutes for construction. During the planning period, you may touch the materials, but you may not prefabricate any parts or arrange the newspaper into different piles. The bricks and the box must remain in the center of the room until the end of the building period. You may go to the bricks and box at any time, however, to test their weight and size."

3. The teacher calls out a two-minute warning before the end of each period. If no bridges have been completed, the teacher may extend the building period for a fixed amount of time, such as five minutes.

4. At the end of the building period, one member of each group tests that group's bridge by passing the box under the bridge and then resting the bricks on the center of the span.

5. The activity should be followed by a five-minute discussion in the groups, with the process observers reporting first. Then the entire class can discuss the activity, focusing on issues such as: how much collaboration and how much competition there was among group members; how the question of leadership was resolved;

what pleased students most; what procedures could be changed so that students might feel more satisfied; whether the groups felt that they were competing against each other. (The teacher should point out that there is no mention of inter-group competition in the instructions.)

6. Students are asked to think back over their behavior during the planning and construction, and to write down two or three changes in their own behavior that they might make if they were to do the activity again. *This is private writing — no one will ask to see these papers.*

NOTE: Students will want to discuss the bridge-building problem and various solutions during the post-building discussion period. This is natural, and the teacher should recognize the validity of this kind of discussion. It is the teacher's job, however, to gently redirect the discussion to the group process of planning and building.

Subject: *Tinker Toys.* [5]

Material: Tinker Toys or other building materials which have a variety of parts, *Process Observer Sheets* (see page 67), pencils.

Procedure:

1. Divide the class into groups of six to eight students with at least one process observer (see page 65) for each

group. Place a box of Tinker Toys in the middle of each group.

2. The teacher instructs the students: "You are to plan and build a structure of Tinker Toys which will be judged for height, stability, beauty, and use of materials. The time limit for the entire activity is sixteen minutes. During the planning period you may talk, but you may not touch the materials. During the building period, you may, of course, touch the materials, but you may not talk with each other or write notes. Your planning period must last at least five minutes and may be no more than ten minutes. After five minutes, you may begin building at any time, but once you start building, you may no longer talk, and you may not go back to the planning stage. I will notify you at the end of five, ten, and fourteen minutes. When I give the signal, the process observer will dump the Tinker Toys out of the box and the timing will begin." The teacher then times the periods.

3. At the end of the building period, groups may examine each other's work, and then the activity should be discussed — first in the small groups, with the process observer commenting first, and then with the entire class.

4. Questions for discussion should be similar to those under "Bridge Building" (above). Additional questions include the following: How should beauty be judged? How well were the group members able to communicate non-

verbally during the building period? How was the time to begin building negotiated? And how did the finished structure differ from each individual's conception of the structure at the end of the planning period?

Notes

1.   For a more complete treatment of this and other related subjects, see Richard A. Schmuck and Patricia A. Schmuck, *Group Processes in the Classroom* (Dubuque, Ia., William C. Brown, 1971).

2.   J. William Pfeiffer and John E. Jones, *A Handbook of Structured Exercises for Human Relations Training*, 3 vols. (Iowa City, Ia., University Associates Press, 1971).

3.   The originator is Jeffrey W. Eiseman.

4.   The originator is David D. Britton.

5.   The originator is David D. Britton.

Chapter Five

ACHIEVEMENT MOTIVATION

Achievement motivation — seemingly a mystical talent or an elusive trick — has been the subject of teachers' anguish and concern for generations. What motivates people to do things — or not do them — is still often a mystery, but in the last dozen years or so, research has begun to throw some light on the subject. We can now make some tentative conclusions about what motivates some students, and what this means for teachers.

First, however, it is important to point out the difference between *motivating* a student and *controlling* him. When a teacher says, "How can I motivate Johnny to do his math?" he may, in fact, be looking for a means of controlling Johnny's behavior. Motivation comes from the inside — all motivation is self-motivation. Somehow Johnny must perceive the task as worth doing, either because of the excitement of making discoveries, or because of the perceived usefulness of the skill or information acquired: pleasing the teacher, earning respect through good grades, avoiding parental disapproval.

Certainly, the more exciting or relevant the task is

perceived to be, the more likely the possibility of motivating the student. At the other extreme, the more arcane or inane the task is perceived to be by the student, the more extreme will be the motivating measures required by the teacher — inducements such as lollipops, transistor radios, days off from school (can you believe it?), or conversely, character defamation and corporal punishment.

Another preliminary consideration is the complexity of motivation. No single motivating force exists within the individual. Motivation is made up of a complex bundle of drives, attitudes, habits, and innate characteristics. Individuals vary in their physiological and psychological make-ups, just as they do in their physical appearances.

INVOLVING THE STUDENTS

With these preliminary considerations of control and individual differences in mind, let us take a look at some of the factors which can contribute to achievement motivation in the classroom. Three general factors establish the motivational climate in the classroom: the *goals* for the class, the *procedures* which are to be used in reaching those goals, and the general *conditions and rules* for work within the classroom. High motivation is more likely present when the goals, procedures, and rules of the class are clearly understood by all, and where the class has participated in formulating these three factors. See page 90 ff. for some ideas as to how the students can become involved in establishing goals, procedures, and rules.

ESTABLISHING GOALS

This does not mean that every class must be planned around the extemporaneous goals laid out by the students. I'm not suggesting that Algebra Two should become a course in sports cars, simply because the students might like it that way, or that Latin One become a seminar on the Beatles. The teacher of Algebra Two can clearly delineate his objectives, both immediate and philosophical, to the class. Within the framework of those goals, however, an attention to the goals of the students — to pass the course, to get a 700 on the College Board Exam, to not be bored — is likely to result in an improved motivational atmosphere in the class.

The one danger in having the students set goals for the class is that the goals may be seen as final and unchanging. As with procedures and rules, goals should be regarded as tentative, capable of being altered in the light of new information or circumstances. Perhaps one of the most important functions of the class should be the continuing re-evaluation of its own goals as the term progresses.

It is also important that goals be seen as realistic and attainable. Students have little motivation to attempt things which they know they will be unable to complete. Achievement motivation generally increases as the challenge increases, but the challenge must be perceived as an invitation to *extend* one's abilities, not as a call to achieve something for which no foundation has been laid.

ESTABLISHING PROCEDURES

In determining the procedures to be used in working toward the goals of the class, two factors are important:

First, students learn in different ways. Each individual will be best motivated if he has a wide variety of learning modes from which to choose.

Second, students generally have an extremely limited view of these possible modes, often thinking that lecturing, reading, memorizing, and directed discussion are the only valid learning procedures. The teacher will need to introduce them to other styles and make clear that learning can take place in unconventional contexts.

Students often believe, for instance, that important learning can take place only when the teacher is present, directing and programming the instruction. They may think of learning only as the acquiring and storing of bits of information for easy retrieval at the teacher's demand. In helping students to expand their concepts of what learning is, the teacher might ask them to discuss how they learned to walk, talk, ride a bicycle, throw a ball, find their way home, buy things with money, operate the television set or record player. The class might try to identify as many people as possible who could be called "teacher" — storekeepers, brothers and sisters, parents, priests, authors, actors, and so on.

Then the teacher might list alternative learning styles — class discussion, lecture, reading and report, large and small group discussion with and without leaders, group independent study, individual independent study, film, group or individual field work, case study, simulation, role play, skits.

And the class can discuss its experiences with each mode, and the possible uses of each for the goals established by the class. Finally, the teacher can set up situations where students can experience those learning styles that they are not familiar with so that they will then be able to choose among a wider range of alternatives.

Two special considerations in establishing procedures are identifying the risks involved in pursuing the goal and structuring tasks so that the risks involved are acceptable to the students. Simply put, any task demands a risk of the student's time, energy, good will, and often his self-esteem. The teacher can help motivate students to take the risks in four ways.

First, he can set clear limits to the size of the risk. For example, if an assignment of ten arithmetic problems seems to involve an unknown quantity of time and effort to a particular student, the teacher might ask this student to spend a limited period of time, such as half-an-hour per night, on the problems. The risk of time and energy is thus clearly limited, and any fears about not completing all the problems have been replaced by the challenge of seeing how many problems he can do accurately in the allotted time.

Second, the teacher can suspend or reduce the threatening consequences of taking a risk. For example, reading one's weekly composition to the whole class may involve the possibility of too great a loss of self-esteem, but reading it in front of a small work group may reduce the risk to an acceptable point.

Third, the teacher can give students permission to take unusual risks, risks that they might hesitate to take without permission. Most students would be reluctant to stand in front of a supermarket and interview the shoppers, for instance; but with a tape recorder in hand and the teacher's "permission," this can be an important learning experience.

Finally, the teacher can show the connection between the risk involved and the consequent reward. Whether it be the joy of a job well done, the usefulness of a new and relevant skill, or a high grade on a report card, whenever the reward is perceived to be important enough to justify the risks, the student will be motivated toward the task.

ESTABLISHING RULES

As to the conditions and rules under which the class will work toward its goals, three factors are particularly relevant. First, where the rules are clear and understandable to all, members of the class are unlikely to be anxious about inadvertently getting into trouble by unintentionally breaking a rule. Second, where the rules and conditions can be seen by the students to be based on the objective requirements of the situation rather than upon the seeming whims of the teacher, the class will be more likely to understand the reasons for the limitations imposed upon them. And third, to the degree that students share in establishing rules and determining the conditions under which they will work, they will be additionally motivated toward the goals of the class.

ESTABLISHING A CLIMATE

One special condition over which the teacher can have some control is in reducing or eliminating the win-lose, highly competitive atmosphere that so often surfaces. Except in specialized cases where competition is perceived as a game, such as in a spelling bee, the aura of competition does little to stimulate even the perennial winners, and adds another layer of threat to those who often lose. Where the grading system requires that students be compared so that some receive A's and some F's on a particular task, then the student's motivation decreases as his expectation of being cast among the losers increases. On the other hand, where tasks are seen as cooperative ventures where each individual can contribute his part and can share in the rewards of the group accomplishment, then motivation, especially the motivation of the less able, tends to increase.

Certainly all of these motivation techniques take time. A question that the teacher must face early in the course is how much time should be diverted from the content of the course into processes such as achievement motivation, fostering open communication, and the like. Most teachers probably devote too little rather than too much time to these useful processes.

Motivation is a diffuse bundle of emotional forces that compel an individual toward action. Ultimately, it is based upon the individual's self-concept and his values, for a person will be emotionally drawn to pursue those goals which he values. The stronger the individual's self-concept and the more positive he is of his abilities, the more likely he is to be motivated to act on his values. Where the individual can see himself engaging in socially significant work, and where the individual can see himself as responsible to himself and to others as a result of that work, he learns to value himself and his ability. He becomes self-motivated.

ACTIVITIES FOR ACHIEVEMENT MOTIVATION

Subject: *Hopes.*

Material: Pencils and paper, tape recorder (if possible).

Procedure:

1.   The teacher asks the students to reflect for four minutes and then write down some of the hopes that each one has for the class over the course of the term (or semester or year). *This is a private writing – the papers will not be collected.*

NOTE: It is important for the teacher to stick to the time set for reflection even though some students may appear to finish early. As students are trained to realize that there really will be time for reflection, many will use the period productively. If the teacher judges that his class wouldn't hold out for four minutes without major disruption, he might set the time for reflection at three, two, or one-and-a-half minutes.

2.   The class is divided into groups of four to six students. Those in each group are given the task of discussing their hopes and preparing a group report which will list some of the group's hopes for the year. Ten minutes is allowed for this task.

3.   At the end of the ten minutes, the teacher calls for group

reports, and each group renders its report in any manner it wishes. The teacher records these reports — by tape recorder if possible — to help him (and his steering committee, if he has one) to plan for the course.

4. The teacher asks the students in the small groups to discuss what things they can do to help realize their hopes, and what things they can do if they see that the class is moving away from the direction of their hopes. This can be followed by a second group report, although one round of group reports is generally enough for one class.

Subject: *Hopes Brainstorm.*

Material: Pencils, paper.

Procedure:

1. The class is divided into small brainstorming groups and the rules of brainstorming (see page 38) are reviewed.

2. The teacher announces a six-minute time period to brainstorm "hopes that we have for the class this year." (This brainstorming can also be done by the entire class with two or three students serving as recorders at the blackboard.)

3. The brainstorming lists are reviewed, and each student is asked to pick out and record the most desirable and the

most ridiculous hope. These hopes are shared with the entire class. This can be followed by discussion either by the class as a whole or in small groups.

Subject: *Hopes Whip.*

Material: None.

Procedure:

1.   Students and teacher are seated in a circle. The teacher asks one person to start by saying, "My hope for this class this year is _____."

2.   Each individual in turn, including the teacher, shares one hope with the class.

3.   This could be followed by an "I hope that I _____" whip which would focus on things that individuals could do to improve the class for themselves.

NOTE: A "whip" is the generic name for any activity where a sentence stem is passed along through the group or class, with each person completing the sentence in turn. The responses should be as spontaneous and unrehearsed as possible, with no stopping for discussion of any response, at least until the whip has been all the way around. Before the whip is started, the teacher should remind the class of their right to pass. "I wonder . . .," "I'm proud that . . .," "I wish . . .," "I believe . . ." are all possible whip stems.

Subject: *Goal Dyads.*

Material: Pencils and paper.

Procedure:

1. Students are asked to reflect individually for three minutes on their goals for the year (term/semester), noting down on paper whatever comes to mind.

2. Pairs are formed, and one person in each pair becomes the focus. He reads off his goals and then the pair discuss things that he can do to help himself toward those goals.

3. After five minutes the focus is changed to the other person and the process is repeated.

4. This may be followed by a class meeting (see page 49) or by *Letters to the Teacher* (see page 97).

Subject: *Topic Brainstorm.*

Material: Chalkboard, pencils, paper.

Procedure:

1. The topic for the next unit of study is announced to the class. Then for seven minutes the class brainstorms questions they would like answered about that topic; all

the questions are listed on the board.

2. The class is divided into groups of four to six. Each
    group spends five minutes selecting three questions
    which are of importance to the group. (More than one
    group may choose the same questions.)

3. The groups are given nine minutes to brainstorm
    questions which arise out of each of the main questions,
    the teacher calling time at the end of three and six
    minutes so that each question gets its share of the
    brainstorming.

4. Each group reports to the entire class.

5. Several courses of action are open at this point: The lists
    can be turned in to the teacher for his evaluation and
    report, a steering committee can be set up to process the
    information and plan future study, or small groups or
    individuals can each select one question for research and
    reporting.

ACTIVITIES FOR FEEDBACK AND MOTIVATION

At a time of life when young people feel powerless over the
use of their time, over the events that shape their lives, over
the metamorphosis that is taking place in their bodies, the
feeling that they have some control over even a small part of
their own education is a powerful motivating force. Formal-
izing the students' need and desire to offer feedback about

their education is a way for the teacher to show he cares what the class thinks and feels, and that he may be willing to change the class to address student needs.

Of course, feedback comes in all the time, whether through teacher-approved channels or not. When a student slouches in his chair, or smiles and nods his head, or stares blankly out the window, or carves on his desk, he's giving informal feedback. While this informal feedback provides important data for the teacher to use in planning and evaluating his work, formal feedback taken at regular intervals is important both to the teacher and to the student.

Subject: *Feedback Forms.*

Material: *Feedback Forms* (see page 96), pencils.

Procedure:

1.   Once a week, the teacher distributes the *Feedback Form* and sets aside ten minutes of class time for students to fill it out and turn it in to the teacher.

2.   On the following day, the teacher summarizes the feedback, noting general trends and pointing out dissenting opinions. The teacher states how he is going to use the feedback, stating what things he can and can't do at this time, noting that change is always a difficult and uncertain thing, and asking for the help, cooperation, and understanding of the class where necessary.

Feedback Form

1. How satisfied were you with this week's sessions? (circle one)

1	2	3	4	5	6	7
VERY						VERY
DISSATISFIED						SATISFIED

2. What was the high point of your week in class?

3. What factors contributed towards your satisfaction?

4. What could be changed to make these sessions better for you?

5. What can I do to make these sessions better for you?

6. What can you do for yourself to make these sessions better for you?

7. What are some of the special issues, concerns, or questions that you would like to see raised in class next week?

8. Free comment/suggestions/questions.

_____

NAME (optional)

Please use the back if you need more space for any item.

Subject: *Feedback Sentence Stems.*

Material: *Feedback Sentence Stems Forms* (see page 99), pencils or pens.

Procedure: Same procedure as Feedback Forms. Some of the sentence stems from this form can also be used as whips.

Subject: *Letters to the Teacher.*

Material: Pencils, pens, paper.

Procedure: Ten or fifteen minutes a week is set aside for students to write a private letter to the teacher. For this activity to be successful, it is important that the teacher make some kind of written answer and return the letters to the students promptly.

CAUTION: Nothing kills this activity faster than commenting on spelling, mechanical errors, handwriting, etc. Some teachers make tape cassettes available to students who wish to talk their letters rather than write them.

Subject: *"Dear Me" Letters.*

Material: Paper, pencils, carbon paper.

Procedure: Once a week, ten or fifteen minutes of class

time is set aside for students to write letters to themselves, making a carbon copy for the teacher. The student keeps the original in a special folder or private notebook.

Subject: *Telegrams.*

Material: Paper, pencils.

Procedure:

1. Five minutes is set aside for students to compose a telegram to the teacher, keeping in mind that telegrams are messages of importance, generally either an instruction to do something, an announcement of an unusual event, or an unusual observation. These telegrams are limited to nine words.

2. The teacher can respond to individual telegrams the next day or write one or two telegrams to the class.

Feedback Sentence Stems Form

1. The high point of my week was when _____

     _____

     _____

2. I feel most satisfied at times when_____

     _____

     _____

3. If I could change one thing about this class it would be

     _____

     _____

4. One thing I'm going to do personally to make these
     classes better for me is _____

     _____

     _____

5. Next week would you please try to_____

     _____

     _____

6.   And I'd also like to say _____

_____

_____

_____

                              _____
                              NAME (optional)

Subject: *Feedback Wall.*

Material: 4 x 6 cards, tape, pencils.

Procedure: A stack of 4 x 6 cards and a roll of tape are always left on a small table placed against the wall. At any time, a student can write a comment or question on one of the cards and place it on the wall. From time to time, the teacher checks the cards on the wall and responds.

Subject: *Feedback Box.*

Material: An appropriate box with a lid, pencils, cards.

Procedure: This is the classic "suggestion box." To be successful, the teacher must open the box at regular intervals and comment on the feedback. If there are no feedback cards in the box, the class should be reminded about the purpose of the box so that they realize that the teacher plans to continue checking the box on a regular basis.

Subject: *Designated Feedback Person.*

Material: Pencil and paper.

Procedure: One member of the class is designated as feedback recipient. Members of the class may bring him their comments and questions at any time, in and out of class. He relays the feedback to the teacher. This job should be rotated through the class, with each student serving two weeks or so.

Subject: *Brainstorm and Rank Order.*

Material: Chalkboard, pencils, paper.

Procedure:

1. The class spends five minutes brainstorming topics which have been covered in class so far. The list is recorded on the board for all to see.

2. The teacher asks the members of the class to select privately the five topics which have been most important to them individually, and then to rank these in order of importance.

3. These lists are shared either with small groups or with the whole class, then turned in to the teacher so he can study and comment on them. Lists to be turned in to the teacher should not be signed unless the student wishes to do so.

Chapter Six

FOSTERING OPEN COMMUNICATION

"We must learn how to improve our communications!" "If only we had been able to communicate better!" "Communications, communications, that's the important thing!" These are the clichés that fly around the room at faculty meeting time. And like all clichés, they touch on a real and important concern. Yet somehow, communication doesn't improve much. The old misunderstandings persist.

More and more English curriculums have become "Communications" curriculums. The content, however, is often much the same — composition focusing heavily on mechanical correctness, literature focusing on an exploration of the deeper meanings of the great works of great authors.

Teachers and administrators are neither villainous nor stupid. Overwhelmingly, they are intelligent and hard-working people who desire to become more effective, but who don't know how to improve their skills in communication.

Communication is a skill at once simple and complex. Basically, it is nothing more than sending and receiving messages. But every message carries with it a certain amount of "noise," extra information often under the conscious control of neither the sender nor the receiver. This information, if perceived, serves to alter the original message. Improving communication involves acquiring an awareness of the variety and scope of this "noise" and skills for reducing or controlling it — for saying what we mean.

Jack Gibb, a social psychologist and originator of the TORI (Trust, Openness, Responsibility, Interdependence) method of interpersonal development, has identified several types of "noise" which produce defensive reactions in receivers and diminish the effectiveness of a communication. He sees communication as a "people process" rather than a "language process"; accordingly, to increase the effectiveness of communication, one must make changes in interpersonal relationships so that the receiver does not feel threatened by the communication. Threat closes the windows of perception and turns the eye inward upon the self, away from the message and sender.

For instance, when a teacher asks, "Where have you been?" the student might feel that this is a genuine request for information based on the teacher's interest in the lives of other people. More likely, however, the student may perceive an implied condemnation of his past behavior. If he does feel threatened, he will start all sorts of defense mechanisms — withdrawal, submission, counterattack — all of which diminish the degree to which he and the teacher can exchange messages rationally and effectively. Furthermore, the student's defensive behavior is likely to raise a defensive posture in the teacher, who then appears more menacing to the student, whose response may again heighten the defensiveness in the teacher in a continuing spiral.

COMMUNICATION CONTINUUMS

Gibb has identified six categories of behavior which tend to raise defensiveness in communication and six contrasting behaviors which lead to open, supportive communication. We have modified Gibb's categories to produce a series of six continuums along which a communication can be rated, from highly defense-producing to highly open and supportive. These continuums are as follows:

Defense-Producing	*Supportive*
Evaluative	Descriptive
Controlling	Cooperative
Hidden	Open
Neutral	Empathetic
Superior	Equal
Certain	Provisional

Evaluative-Descriptive: Messages — both verbal and non-verbal — which appear to evaluate the listener are defense-raising. The put-down is a good example of a highly evaluative kind of communication which is popular among students: "Wouldn't you know it?" or "That's just like you!" or "Nice going." Or non-verbally, hitting the forehead with the butt of the palm and rolling the eyes.

But there are other forms of evaluative communication that are more subtle. Statements of value judgment often are inferred by the receiver to be evaluative, that is, appreciating the receiver for agreement, depreciating him for non-agreement; for instance: "I think all this recycling business is nonsense," or "Anyone who voted for Gene McCarthy is a hopeless idealist." Many questions, too, imply evaluation in that the responder will be judged on the basis of whether his answer conforms with the questioner's expectations.

At the descriptive end of the continuum are those messages which present feelings, ideas, or facts, but which do not imply that the receiver should change his attitudes or behavior. "I" statements are generally descriptive rather than evaluative. "I feel upset with your behavior," or "I feel that I need more information before I can decide about that" describe the sender's condition while "You're making me upset," or "You haven't told me what I need to know" evaluate the other's actions.

Controlling-Cooperative: Messages which are perceived as attempts to influence the receiver's attitudes, change his behavior, or restrict his activities are defense-raising. And while an overt attempt at control elicits either acceptance or open rejection, the more subtle the controlling message is perceived to be, the greater the degree of defensiveness and resentment. "Don't you all want to do well in your next school?" "I'm sure everybody really wants to do well on the test." "Didn't we agree at the beginning of the year that we wouldn't chew gum in class?" These are all transparent attempts to control values or behavior.

When the message indicates a desire on the part of the

sender to engage in a cooperative enterprise, then the message generally creates the same spirit of cooperation in the receiver. The cooperative message implies a willingness on the part of the sender to allow the receiver to set his own goals, make his own decisions, and evaluate his own progress, or else to collaborate with the sender in the process: "What's the best way to handle this?" or "How do you want to divide up the research for this report?" or "Let's see how we can work this out," or "What can I do to help you finish this composition?"

Hidden-Open: When the receiver feels that the message is ambiguous or has a hidden purpose, he naturally raises his defenses. This is especially true when the receiver feels that the sender is using some kind of strategy to make the receiver think he is making his own decisions. Psychologists who set up a test which ostensibly tests for one thing while secretly testing for something else often find a resentment when the subject discovers the hidden purpose. And teachers who ask students to bring in rock music to listen to, and then force the class to write a composition about it can be resented for the same reason. No one likes to be tricked.

At the other end of the continuum, a message which is seen as open and uncomplicated is likely to reduce the defensiveness of a receiver. When the purposes of the message sender are clear, the receiver becomes more open to the message. In a classroom context, the teacher who is clear about his goals, and about why he is asking students to follow certain procedures, is the most likely to elicit student cooperation.

Neutral-Empathetic: When the tone or content of the

message reveals no concern for the welfare of the receiver, the receiver wonders why he is not valued by the sender, and inevitably becomes defensive. The teacher who hides all emotion generates an uncaring feeling among students toward the teacher. This impairs his ability to teach, and the students' ability to learn.

In contrast, where the message sender conveys a feeling of empathy and caring towards the receiver, the receiver feels supported, and his defenses are not erected. Teachers who show their concern for the personalities and welfare of their students engender feelings of trust and responsiveness in their students. This reciprocity works to the advantage of both.

Superior-Equal: The message receiver who feels that the sender is communicating to him from a position of superiority — in intellectual ability, power, wealth, social position, physical strength, whatever — will put up defenses to prevent his being "shown up." In a class where the teacher makes a difficult problem look easy for himself to do, the students often react by feeling less worthy or by tuning out the teacher's message. And when the teacher uses his position of power to force the students to do something "because I say so," the students cannot help resenting him for rubbing their noses in the fact of their powerlessness.

Real differences in power or status do exist, but the effective message sender is the one who creates a climate where these differences do not seem to be an important part of the relationship. If the person with high power or status is perceived to be willing to engage in mutual problem-solving and in a give-and-take of ideas, the receiver is more open to his messages.

Certain-Provisional: The message sender who seems absolutely certain of his correctness, who knows all the answers, who needs no help or additional information, is a well-known defense producer. The teacher who is never wrong, or must always have an answer for everything, blocks himself off from his students, makes it apparent to his students that they can have no effect on him. Thus he raises their feelings of powerlessness and hence, their defenses.

On the other hand, the message sender who shows that he is interested in experimenting, in finding answers, in problem-solving and exploring, in gaining new information, communicates a willingness to share with others. And this in turn engenders a feeling of openness and support from others.

Taken together, the six categories at the right-hand end of the continuum represent an attractive personality type — descriptive, cooperative, open, empathetic, equal, provisional — while the six categories at the left represent quite another — evaluative, controlling, hidden, neutral, superior, certain. Clearly, few people could be characterized by all six of the undesirable and unproductive traits. But teachers who want to become more effective communicators can pick one or two areas where they see themselves near the defense-raising end of the continuum, and then try different behaviors which might move them toward the other end of that continuum.

THREE POINTERS TO BETTER COMMUNICATION

Looking at communication from another angle, we have found three pointers tremendously useful in understanding this complex process. The first is that *almost every question has a statement underlying it.* Take a simple question such as "What did you think of that movie?" This could really be saying, "I want you to commit yourself first so that I can agree with you and earn your esteem," or "I'm really puzzled by the movie," or "I want to know if you are as good a critic as I am," or "I'm embarrassed by silence, let's talk," or many more things. By phrasing the statement as a question, the questioner has forced the listener to try to determine which of the possible underlying statements he should respond to.

One way to improve communication is to become more aware of what our concerns really are when we ask a question, and to try to identify those concerns to our listeners as fully as possible. Another way to improve communication is to listen for questions which might reflect underlying concerns of others, and then to ask for clarification of the concerns which underlie the questions.

A second useful pointer is to identify *introjectors* — those questions and statements which try to force a value position on another person: "We all can agree that civil defense is important, can't we?" or "But don't you believe that the home is the most important influence in the early years?" or "I think that we are all agreed that everyone should do some work for the sake of his own self-esteem." These are verbal strongarm tactics which, while they may gain overt acceptance or agreement, often lead to underlying resentment. Changing these to "I" statements is more likely to lead to an open exchange of ideas, less likely to raise defensiveness.

The third pointer is to *be aware of put-downs or killer statements*: "You don't really mean that, do you?" or "How many times do I have to tell you?" or "Can't you get it right just this once?" or "Not that way, stupid!" These statements are defense-raising because they attack the person rather than the problem.

The most common response of a person who has been assaulted by a put-down is to look for deficiencies in the personality of the one who put him down. The receiver and sender become locked in an ego conflict, attacking each other's personalities rather than engaging in a cooperative approach to solving a problem. The eventual outcome of such an encounter is likely to be one of three possibilities: continued hostility, retreat and withdrawal on the part of one of the persons, or submission of one to the other. Even though one person may eventually gain his will over the other, no one benefits.

Being aware of put-downs and killer statements is perhaps the most important step in making the climate of the classroom open and supportive. Young people are masters of the put-down. They learn it from their peers, from their adult acquaintances, from television; and they use it unsparingly on each other without recognizing the unwitting damage that they may be doing to others and themselves. The teacher can foster an awareness of put-downs in many ways: by discussion and explanation, by brainstorming all the possible verbal put-downs that students can think of and then all the non-verbal ones, by role playing situations where one person is trying to put down another, or by asking students to keep a record of all the put-downs they hear in the course of a morning. Then through discussion and role play, the class can identify and try out ways of dealing with put-downs so as not to get revenge but to channel energy toward solving problems.

ACTIVITIES FOR FOSTERING OPEN COMMUNICATION

Subject: *Accident Report.*[1]

Material: *Accident Report Worksheets* (see page 113), pencils, tape recorder if possible.

Procedure:

1. Six volunteers play the part of the report chain. They are given numbers, one through six, and sent out of the room.

2. The teacher distributes the *Accident Report Worksheets* to the rest of the class. He reads over the accident report with the class, and explains the procedure: that he will call in the first member of the report chain and read him the accident report; the first member of the report chain will call in the second member and retell the report to the best of his ability; then the second member calls in the third, and so on until all have been called in and heard the report from the person just ahead on the report chain.

3. As each member reports to the next on the chain, the rest of the class note on their *Accident Report Worksheets* any changes in the new version from the previous report.

4. As soon as the sixth member of the report chain repeats

the accident report (to the teacher and class), the teacher reads the initial report once more.

5. A large group discussion of the exercise follows. Focus should be on the difficulty of transferring information accurately, and on ways to improve one's ability to transfer information. The initial focus should be on the reactions of the six members of the reporting chain, and on their feelings as they tried to concentrate on the message. It is important that the members not be subjected to blame or ridicule for faulty transmission of information. As a skill-building exercise, the class might repeat the activity with a new set of volunteers and a new accident report.

Accident Report Worksheet

Message: "Please listen carefully, for I must leave. I have just called the police from the gas station on the corner. Wait here and report the accident to them. As I was crossing the intersection, I saw the milk truck, which was heading west, start to make a right-hand turn when the estate wagon, heading east, started to turn left. Both brake lights flashed on at the same time. The wagon's wheels must have locked, because it went straight ahead into the side of the truck."

Directions: For each repetition of the report, note any additions, subtractions, or distortions from the previous report.

First repetition:

Second repetition:

Third repetition:

Fourth repetition:

Fifth repetition:

Sixth repetition:

Subject: *Architects and Builders.*[2]

Material: Sets of building materials such as Tinker Toys, Leggo, or soda straws and tape.

Procedure:

1. The teacher has pre-built a structure from one set of the material and the structure is hidden behind a screen or in a closet.

2. Students are divided into groups of six, and each group is given a set of the materials.

3. The groups divide into sub-groups of three designated as sub-group A and sub-group B. *After* the sub-groups have determined which will be A and which will be B, the teacher announces that A's will be architects and B's will be builders.

4. Architects are to go to the structure the teacher has pre-built and examine it carefully for two or three minutes. Builders are to take their materials to a place where they will have room to work, and examine them.

5. On a signal from the teacher, the architects return to their builders and instruct the builders in replicating the hidden structure. During the seven-minute building period, the builders may not talk to each other or to the architects. The architects may return to the original structure to check details as often as they wish.

6. At the end of the seven minutes, the architects and builders check their structures against the teacher's, and score themselves, allowing one point for each piece of material which is correctly placed.

7. The class discusses the activity, focusing first on the feelings of the builders and then on the feelings of the architects.

8. The class may wish to repeat the activity with the architects and builders switching roles. Of course, a new model must be readied behind the screen for the second trial.

Subject: *Communication Cards.*

Material: 4 x 6 cards, six per student, twelve for the teacher.

Procedure:

1. This is similar to "Architects and Builders" except that it is done in pairs. In each pair, one person is designated sender and the other, receiver.

2. The teacher arranges one set of 4 x 6 cards so that each card touches the next at some point (see diagram on page 116).

3. The sender is allowed to observe this pattern and make a diagram for himself. He then goes to his receiver and tells the receiver how to arrange the cards to duplicate the

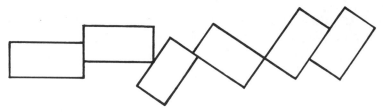

original pattern. It is useful to apply a time limit for the task so that all can go on to the next task at the same time.

4.   The following conditions can be imposed by the teacher to show the difficulty of various types of communication:

    a.   One way: Only the sender may talk.

    b.   Blind sender: The sender sits with his back to the receiver so that he cannot see the cards as the receiver arranges them.

    c.   One way with blind sender: Like blind sender, except that the receiver may not talk. Receiver may tap the sender when he is ready for further instructions.

    d.   Written: For this variation, both can be receivers and senders. The teacher sets out two patterns of cards, one at each end of the room. Pairs divide, half of each going to opposite ends of the room, where they write instructions for arranging cards like the pattern at that end of the room (time limit, five minutes). Members of each pair then exchange written instructions and return to their own ends, where they attempt to reproduce the pattern at the opposite end on the basis of their partners' instructions.

5. This activity is followed by a discussion of communication, the importance of audio and visual feedback, and the uses of defining terms and identifying reference points.

Subject: *Human Knots.*

Material: None.

Procedure:

1. The class is divided into groups of four. One person is designated as instructor, the other three as students.

2. While the instructor closes his eyes, the three students hold hands to form a circle, then twist and weave themselves into a human knot. Students must not let go of each other's hands.

3. The instructor opens his eyes and directs the students specifically about how to unwind.

4. The entire class comes back together for a discussion, allowing the instructors to speak first, then the students. The activity may be repeated with new instructors.

NOTE: It is probably best not to use this activity unless there is good community and a joyful sense of purpose within the class.

Subject: *Blind Puzzle.*

Material: Simple jigsaw puzzles such as preschoolers might use — one puzzle for each four people, blindfolds, paper bags.

Procedure:

1. Class is divided into groups of four. Each group sits around a small table or desk. One student is designated as the instructor, the other three as students. The three students put on blindfolds (or merely close their eyes). The teacher places a paper bag containing the mixed-up puzzle on each table.

2. At a signal from the teacher, the instructor turns over the bag and allows the pieces to fall out on the table. From this point on, the instructor may not touch the pieces.

3. The instructor tells the students how to assemble the puzzle. The activity can continue until all the puzzles are complete, or a time limit can be imposed and points scored for each piece of the puzzle successfully in place.

4. Debriefing first in small groups, then with the entire class.

Subject: *Yes, Robert, No, Susan.*

Material: Same as for "Blind Puzzle."

Procedure:

1. This is a more difficult version of the "Blind Puzzle." After the bags have been dumped on the table, there is an initial instruction period of one minute where only the instructor may talk while the students remain silent and blindfolded.

2. After the one-minute instruction period, the instructor may say only the words *yes* and *no* and the names of the students. A time limit is generally desirable.

3. The activity should be followed by small group and class debriefing. "I Learned . . ." Statements (see page 143) may be called for.

Subject: *Catch the Cup.*

Material: Aluminum saucepans; unbreakable cups or other objects of similar size and weight, such as wooden blocks or hockey pucks; blindfolds.

Procedure:

1. The teacher demonstrates the activity by placing a cup

on the bottom of an overturned saucepan, flipping the cup in the air and then turning the saucepan up to catch the cup. (This is a fairly simple task, but the teacher may wish to practice a bit before class.)

2. Two volunteers are called for. One becomes the student, the other the instructor. The student is blindfolded and the instructor gives him the inverted saucepan and places the cup on top of the pan.

3. The instructor teaches the student to flip and catch the cup. For the lesson to be thoroughly learned, the student must catch the cup three times in a row. It may be necessary to place a time limit on this activity.

4. After the student completes the "lesson," the instructor is blindfolded and given three chances to catch the cup without instruction.

5. The activity is discussed, concentrating on those aspects of the communication which were most effective in the learning process, and noting what assumptions the instructor may have made which were unjustified in the light of his own trials.

6. This activity can be done with one pair and the rest of the class observing, two pairs with the rest of the class divided into two circles, or one pair observing each pair (or the two pairs can be competing). If enough pans and cups can be gathered together, everyone can take part.

Subject: *Blind Landing.*

Material: Blindfold, assorted obstacles.

Procedure:

1. One volunteer is designated "Pilot" and another is "Control Tower."

2. The remaining students form two lines facing each other, about four feet apart. The area between the two lines is the "runway" which the Pilot must successfully negotiate blindfolded.

3. Pilot is blindfolded and then books, shoes, etc., are scattered along the runway as obstacles which Control Tower must guide Pilot through.

4. Pilot starts at one end of the runway, Control Tower stands at the other and gives instructions to the Pilot. The Pilot-Control Tower team gets one crash-point for every obstacle touched (including persons lining the edge of the runway).

5. Other controls which can be imposed are one-way communication, where the Pilot may not talk back to the Control Tower; yes-no communication, where the Pilot asks questions about his course while the Control Tower is limited to saying yes and no; timed runs, where a time limit of three minutes is imposed on the landing.

A tape recording of the activity gives helpful feedback, especially to the Control Tower.

6. After the landing, a general debriefing is held with focus on questions such as the following: What directions seemed most helpful, least helpful? How did the Control Tower gain the confidence of the Pilot? Is this confidence a necessary aspect of the problem? How well were terms defined, and how could they be better defined? What is the difference between one-way and two-way communication?

Subject: *Focus Listening.*

Material: None.

Procedure:

1. "Focus Listening" can be used for groups of three or four or for the whole class (seated in a circle). A topic is chosen for discussion and one person volunteers to be the focus person. That person is given a certain amount of time to talk about the subject for discussion. It's best to start with a short, non-threatening time limit such as a minute and a half, and to build up gradually as students get the knack of asking clarifying and extending questions.

2. Others in the group must try to understand what that

person is saying by asking clarifying or extending questions where necessary, but under no circumstances changing the focus to another person by a statement such as "That reminds me of the time when I . . ." or by a question such as "Did you ever try that with onions? I always used to . . ."

3. For groups of more than four, one person should be designated as the process observer to insure that the focus is maintained on the focus person. The process observer should call out "Foul!" loudly whenever he sees the focus shifting to someone else.

4. At the end of each focus round, students are asked to reflect for a moment about how well they listened, how much they can recall about what the focus person was actually saying.

5. Then the focus shifts, and a new topic for discussion can be used if desired. (Note that if the same topic is to be used, students should be warned about the temptation to rehearse their turn instead of listening to the focus person.) Any positive focus topic is good to start with — one happy moment from earlier childhood, the one day I'd like to live over and do exactly the same thing, the place I'd most like to live for a whole year (not my present home), my sports or TV hero, etc. Discussions of rank orders (page 151), a person's position on forced-choice games (page 155), or personal inventories (page 61 ff.) are also good topics.

Subject: *Communication Guidelines Rank Order.*

Material: *Communication Guidelines Sheets* (see below) pencils.

Procedure:

1. Each student, working independently, ranks the "Communication Guidelines" as he feels they are important for effective communication, from most important for effective communication (number 1) to least important for effective communication (number 8).

2. The class divides into groups of four or five. Each group tries to reach consensus on the rank order.

3. After ten minutes, each group reports to the entire class.

Communication Guidelines Sheet

1. *Be aware of the "here and now" — what you are feeling and thinking at this instant.*   When you're feeling sad, you respond differently to a communication than when you're feeling happy. What you feel affects both the transmission and the reception of the message.

2. *It is more useful to talk to a person than about him.*   Being open about areas of agreement and disagreement is more productive than trying to work behind someone's back.

3. *Be aware of your own personal "filters" — predisposi-tions to take a side before all the evidence is in.* Filters such as being a Red Sox fan, being a Republican, being a women's liberation advocate, or being a student, tend to screen information so that a person sees only the side which supports his established position.

4. *Be aware of "people should" or "everyone ought to" statements.* These can be a way of shifting responsi-bility from yourself to "society" (hence, nothing can be done). Try using "I" statements in their place.

5. *Be aware that most questions have an underlying statement behind them.* It is often more useful to identify the statement and say that, instead of saying the question. "Where did you go?" may be a legitimate question or it may mean, "I am concerned that you might have been doing something that I would not approve of — tell me what it was."

6. *Be aware of trying to impose your views on others by using introjectors.* Such phrases as "Don't you believe . . . ?" or "Wouldn't you agree . . . ?" or "Every-one knows that . . ." subtly attempt to introject your views into someone else's value system.

7. *Be aware of killer statements — those statements which act as put-downs.* "You don't really believe that, do you?" "Come on, you've got to be kidding." "Where did you get that idea?" "That's *some* necktie." And on and on and on. The victim may laugh and all may consider it just another joke, but very often there is a residue of

hurt or resentment or threat, all of which close down the windows of perception and hinder communication.

8. *Openness and truth are not valuable in their own right.* Communication is impaired when a receiver feels attacked or threatened by an open or truthful statement.

Subject: *Communication Climate Inventory.*

Material: *Communication Climate Inventory* (see page 128), pencils or pens.

Procedure:

1. The *Inventory* is distributed to each member of the class.

2. The teacher discusses briefly each of the aspects represented in the six continuums.

3. Students are asked to identify a recent communication and to rate that communication along the six continuums.

4. The class has a general discussion of supportive and defense-raising communication.

5. An alternate procedure is to ask the students to rank-order the six continuums, first individually and then in consensus-seeking groups, as with the "Communications Guidelines."

The lower the total score, the more likely the communication has produced a defensive climate and rejection by the receiver. The higher the total score, the more likely the communication has produced a supportive climate and acceptance by the receiver.

To improve your communication patterns, pick one or two items where you feel your communication would be rated as defense-raising. Then brainstorm ways to modify your behavior so that your communication will be perceived as more supportive.

Subject: *Body Language Awareness.*

Material: Television set or video-tape recorder and playback device.

Procedure:

1. Turn the television set on to a picture showing a close-up of actors.

2. Turn the sound off and ask the class to spend two minutes observing all of the gestures and body positions which communicate messages.

3. At the end of two minutes, turn the picture off and hold a general discussion of what was noted.

4. Repeat this procedure several times, as each new viewing

will reveal new insights into body language.

Subject: *Be the Picture.*

Material: Several pictures of human beings engaging in some kind of activity.

Procedure:

1.   The picture is shown to the entire group and comments are elicited as to the body language which is evidenced.

2.   The class is divided into pairs. One person from each pair is to be the picture — that is, assume a posture and facial expression exactly the same as the person in the picture. His partner compares him with the real picture and helps him to become as much like the picture as possible.

3.   Roles are reversed and the second person tries to be the picture.

4.   A general discussion of body language follows.

Communication Climate Inventory [3]

Directions: Below are six continuums which represent aspects of a communication climate. Circle the number on each of the six continuums that is the closest to the way you feel about the communication in question. Then total the results.

DEFENSIVE   SUPPORTIVE

Evaluative: The receiver   1 2 3 4 5 6 7 *Descriptive*
feels that he is being
evaluated by the sender.

Controlling: The receiver   1 2 3 4 5 6 7 *Cooperative*
feels that the sender is
attempting to control the
receiver's behavior.

Hidden: The receiver   1 2 3 4 5 6 7   *Open*
feels that the sender is
tricking him or pulling
a strategy on him.

Neutral: The receiver   1 2 3 4 5 6 7 *Empathetic*
feels that the sender is
lacking concern for the
receiver's welfare.

Superior: The receiver   1 2 3 4 5 6 7   *Equal*
feels that the sender has
judged the receiver to be
inferior.

Certain: The receiver   1 2 3 4 5 6 7 *Provisional*
feels that the sender is
not open to any position
except the one he is
espousing.

TOTAL SCORE _____

ACTIVITIES FOR NON-VERBAL COMMUNICATION AND SENSORY AWARENESS

Many of the activities above have involved some form of non-verbal communication. The activities which follow are primarily concerned with fostering open communication on a non-verbal level and with heightening awareness of one's self and one's senses. Most of the activities below should be presented only when there is healthy trust, a feeling of community, and a sense of purpose in the class.

The teacher must trust that non-verbal learning will take place non-verbally. Although the effect of the activities can be heightened by discussion, an exhaustive clinical analysis following each activity is probably counterproductive. Play it by ear: raise issues and questions and allow the discussion to flow with the interest of the students.

Subject: *Mirror Dance.*

Material: Record player or tape recorder with rock or other rhythmic music.

Procedure:

1. Students pair off and designate one member of each pair as *A* and the other as *B*. It is not necessary to pair off with someone of the opposite sex, as students will not be dancing together.

2. The teacher starts the music, and all dance and move rhythmically.

3. Periodically, the teacher stops the music. Have a screen in front of the record player so that students will not know when. When the music stops, the dancers must freeze in position. Everyone can look at the others, trying not to move.

4. Then the teacher directs: "B's keep on freezing; A's, find your partner, face him, and be his mirror — try to make your whole body look exactly like he looks."

5. The music resumes and the dancers continue as before until the music stops again.

NOTE: The teacher might stop the music two or three times first without mirroring so that students get used to freezing. Then the mirroring can be added. A prepared tape with random silences will allow the teacher to move away from the machine.

Subject: *Adverbs.*

Material: 3 x 5 cards with adverbs printed on one side.

Procedure:

1.   The teacher should prepare a deck of adverb cards by writing one adverb on one side of each card: tenderly, quickly, urgently, slowly, blankly, demandingly, meekly, etc. (The class might brainstorm adverbs in preparation for this.)

2.   The deck is shuffled. One student picks a card and goes out of the room. He reads the card and then comes back into the room, behaving in the manner of the adverb. He may use any props that are convenient.

3.   After twenty seconds, students may start guessing the adverb.

Subject: *The Big Machine.*

Material: None.

Procedure:

1.   Ask the class: "If you could be part of a big machine, what part would you like to be?" One student volunteers to start the machine, comes out to the middle of the floor, and starts moving as part of the machine might.

2. When other students see how they might fit, they join the machine, moving in relationship to each other. If their part makes a certain noise, they may make that noise.

NOTE: Big machines always stop themselves naturally; there is no need for the teacher to step in. The teacher may take part in the big machine if he wishes. No one should be forced to be a part of the big machine: observing is almost as rewarding as participating.

Here are some questions for discussion: To what extent did the part you played represent the part you play in the real world? To what extent were you aware of the total machine? Were you conscious of the evaluation of others? Were you competing to be more creative than others? Were you concerned that you might be judged less creative than others? What other here-and-now feelings can you recall?

Subject: *Blind Walk.*

Material: Blindfolds.

Procedure:

1. Students form pairs. One will be the leader, the other the led. The person led will close his eyes or be blindfolded.

2. The leader leads his partner on a walk, trying to give him a rich sensory experience, but at the same time creating in him trust in his guide. The leader must be careful not

to let his blind partner fall or bump into things. The leader may lead anywhere that is customarily permitted or where the teacher has made special arrangements. He must be especially careful on stairs.

3. After ten minutes, reverse roles so that the leader becomes the led. Repeat the activity for another ten minutes.

NOTE: The blind walk can be conducted entirely within the classroom if necessary, but the time limit should probably be lowered. Students should be left to themselves to decide how the leading is going to be done (by voice, hand, arm, etc.), which is to go first, whether or not to wear a blindfold (some persons find it uncomfortable to hold their eyes closed for long periods).

Issues for discussion include the following: trust in self, trust in others, sense awareness, notions of time and space, learning, communication, negotiating the method of leading and whether to wear a blindfold or not.

Notes

1. Pfeiffer and Jones, *op. cit.*

2. Schmuck and Schmuck, *op. cit.*

3. Based on "Defensive Communication," by Jack Gibb in *Interpersonal Dynamics*, Warren Bennis et al. eds. (Homewood, Illinois, The Dorsey Press, 1968).

Chapter Seven

INFORMATION SEEKING, GATHERING, AND SHARING

Many of us subscribe to more magazines than we can read and have a "must read" list that grows ever longer. Through our newspapers, we are daily assailed with more information than we can possibly absorb. Yet for all our modern methods of disseminating information, our methods of processing information remain primitive and inefficient. Furthermore, our schools seem to be locked into a conspiracy to limit the variety, quantity, and sources of information available to students. The use of textbooks, for example, insures that all students will get the same limited amount of information on a given subject, and will have little opportunity to verify that information with other sources. The practice of having the entire class read the same poem, the same novel, the same short story, limits the variety of cultural and aesthetic information available in the classroom; this reverence for certain "classics" reinforces an artificial conception of cultural unity. Furthermore, these practices have the effect of making students less valuable to each other as resources.

This is not to deny the value of some common assignments. Classes often work more effectively together when there is some common body of knowledge. What is needed is flexibility.

COLLABORATIVE INFORMATION PROCESSING

In a world where we are threatened with being swamped and confused and misled by information overload, one of the most important skills which we can teach our children is collaborative information processing. What is overwhelming to one may be comprehensible to a group. Part of the path to knowledge lies in learning how to discard those pieces of information which are not relevant so that the remaining pieces can be formed into a comprehensible pattern.

Effective leaders in industry, politics, and the military almost always rely on teams of aides who collect and organize information from both inside and outside the organization.

The classroom can be a training ground for shared information processing based on a trust in each member as a gatherer and sorter of information. This kind of process training can also help young.people to become more aware of their need for interdependence in accomplishing many of their individual goals. It can help them to form a realistic sense of what they can expect from different sorts of people, so that they can maintain a balance between unwisely trusting incompetent sources and being unwisely suspicious of helpful and competent ones.

One way to teach this kind of information processing is to ask the class to work in small problem-solving groups. Whether it's a page of rate-time-distance problems, a series of sonnets from Shakespeare, or a sequence of lines from Vergil, groups of four or five students can work together and then make short reports to the class.

If three important novels represent a certain theme or period, the class can be divided into three groups, each group reading one of the novels. Then, after completing the books, or at various stages during the reading, the groups hold discussions about their novels. The other members of the class listen to the discussion and ask questions.

ASSESSING THE LEVEL OF INFORMATION PRESENT

Another possibility is for the teacher to ask the class, "What do you know, and what do you want to know?" Regardless of subject (the Pilgrims' first Thanksgiving, the anatomy of a frog, the concept of prejudice), the teacher asks the class to brainstorm all the things that they know about the subject, with the teacher or volunteer students noting each item on the board. After four or five minutes, the teacher asks the students to reflect individually on what things they would like to know in addition. After allowing a minute or two for reflection, the teacher writes the students' questions on the board.

When a list of ten or twelve questions has been gathered, there are a number of things that the class can do. The teacher may ask the class to look over the list to see if there are any questions that individuals in the class might be able to answer or shed light on. This often produces some information from students who have special knowledge or insights in the field. Then the teacher might ask each student to choose one question that is most interesting to him. Those who have chosen the same question may either form work groups or work independently, and report back to the class on their research.

In asking "What do you know, and what do you want to know?" the teacher may find that certain pieces of misinformation appear among the items "known," but he should write down every item no matter how inaccurate it may be. There are several reasons for this. First, if the teacher serves as an instant arbiter of what shall be placed on the board and what shall not, some students may be reluctant to volunteer for fear of being put down. Second, it is important to know if misinformation does exist in the class, and to what extent. Third, many pieces of information may appear incorrect from the teacher's perspective but later become valid perceptions through supporting evidence from the students. Finally, this misinformation can be structured into a learning opportunity: at the end of the brainstorming, the teacher may ask the students to look over the list of things that they know and see if there are any items that they might disagree with. If disagreements arise, then each proponent may be asked to state his position, and the teacher can ask for some independent research. The lesson is thus expanded to include ways of finding and verifying information. On the other hand, if no one questions an erroneous item, the teacher may say, "Hmmm—1491. My impression is that the date was 1492. How can we find out who's right?"

If learning how to learn is one of the primary goals of formal education, then information processing — seeking, gathering, organizing, and sharing — is a vital skill. It is little practiced in the traditional classroom where the teacher and his prescribed textbooks are viewed as the fount of knowledge. Any activity or pattern of teaching that demonstrates the effectiveness of collaboration in the processing of information will increase a student's chances of coping with the flood of information outside the classroom.

ACTIVITIES FOR INFORMATION PROCESSING

Subject: *Brainstorming to Teach Organization.*

Material: Blackboard, chalk.

Procedure:

1. The class is given a topic and asked to brainstorm items that could go under the main heading.

2. One of these items is selected, and the class brainstorms subheadings under that item. The process can be repeated until the sub-subheadings (or the students) are exhausted.

   Example:

   Subject: Cars

   Items: Engine, body, uses, colors, makes, etc.

   Subheads of Engine: Fuel, carburetor, pistons, exhaust, etc.

   Subheads of Fuel: Octane, additives, brands, etc.

Subject: *High-Tension Wire.*

Material: None.

Procedure:

1. In the Outward Bound program, one group task is to get all members of the group over a simulated high-tension wire. If one member of the group touches the wire, the group fails. This concept can be introduced to the class and then applied to any skill — learning multiplication tables, performing square roots, punctuating with semi-colons, memorizing parts of a frog. Rather than attempt to develop the skill on an individual basis, use the power of the group to help each other so that all can get over the "high-tension wire" — the test.

2. Divide the class into groups of four or five, being sure that all the "brains" are not together, and set the groups to the job of "getting over the wire."

Subject: *Role Plays and Simulations.*

Material: None.

Procedure: Historical and social situations can be role played or simulated (see "The Leader and the Led," on page 75, for example). Also, different persons can role play parts of the body (one the heart, one the blood, one the kidney, etc.). Furthermore, a simulation or role play can be used to heighten the experiencing of a work of literature.

Subject: *Forced-Choice Games and Rank Orders.*

Material: Paper and pencil.

Procedure:

1. The class brainstorms the causes of the Civil War (the teacher supplies any important ones that are missing).

2. The students break up into small groups and rank order these causes in order of importance. Each student shares his rankings with others in his group, which tries to arrive at a consensus ranking. By working over the material in this way, the students will incidentally learn the items on the list.

NOTE: All of the activities in this book can be used effectively as vehicles for practicing a foreign language. Whether to do the entire activity in the foreign tongue or to do part in English depends upon the achievement level of the particular class. For example, a group studying French could read "The Marijuana Story" (see page 180) in English, discuss it in English or French, and then make up a report, either written or oral, in French for the rest of the class.

Subject: *Card Lecturette.*

Material: 3 x 5 cards, pencils.

Procedure:

1. Ask the class to prepare a lecturette by brainstorming all

they know about the given subject (the reason the Pilgrims left England, the functions of the lymph gland, the concept of sets, etc.).

2.   Distribute 3 x 5 cards to each small group of students.

3.   The students decide which are the most important items, and write them down — one to a card.

4.   The cards are then organized and used as the basis of notes for the lecturette, which one person in the group will deliver.

Subject: *Skill Rounds.*

Material: Short problems in math, language, etc.

Procedure:

1.   Students are seated in groups of threes or fours. All work on the same math problem, or some sentence to translate, or other task.

2.   At the end of one minute, they pass their papers to the right and compare their work with that of the next person; then they pass the papers to the right once more and check again.

3.   Disparities are discussed within the group, and the teacher calls for a correct answer.

4. The round is repeated with a new problem.

Subject: *"I Learned . . ." and "I Believe . . ." Statements.*[1]

Material: Pencils, paper.

Procedure:

1. "I learned . . ." and "I believe . . ." Statements are particularly useful to help students develop the ability to summarize and draw inferences from the material elicited by the activity just completed. At the end of an activity or discussion, ask the students to write one or two "I learned . . ." Statements (if the activity focuses on learning about one's self) or "I believe . . ." Statements (if the activity focuses on clarifying values and positions on issues). It should be made clear that students will not be compelled to share these statements with anyone, although they may do so if they wish.

2. After students have had a minute or two to frame their statements, the teacher asks if anyone would like to share his statements with the class. This sharing should take place in an atmosphere of acceptance, and therefore it is often better not to open the floor for discussion of an individual's "I learned . . ." or "I believe . . ." Statements.

   Below are some additional sentence stems in the same spirit. Notice that for the "I learned . . ." Statements, the second "I" directs the learner's attention to things that he has learned about himself:

> "I learned that I . . ."
>
> "I re-learned that I . . ."
>
> "I noticed that I . . ."
>
> "I was pleased that I . . ."
>
> "I believe . . ."
>
> "I stand for . . ."
>
> "I cherish . . ."
>
> "I am proud of . . ."

Notes

1. The originator is Sidney B. Simon.

Chapter Eight

VALUE EXPLORATION AND CLARIFICATION[1]

All of us are continually faced with situations which involve making a conscious choice: Shall I get up and get a pencil? Shall I bother to read further? Shall I grade papers this afternoon, or read a book, or go shopping, or . . .?

Moreover, as teachers, we see our students faced with a bewildering array of choice situations, choices concerning sex, family, friends, work, leisure, money, religion, time, self-appraisal, and many more. And there is growing evidence that as the number of choices becomes overpowering, certain learning problems arise: the under-achiever, the apathetic or inconsistent student, the drifter, the reflexive rebel. These "problem students" often suffer from a sense of alienation from their own feelings, a lack of clarity in decision making, a *confusion of values.*

Where are the guideposts to help in these choice situations? To what extent are the *shoulds* which we have given our young people through family, church, and school realistic to them? What part of our young people's lives are spent in trying to reconcile those *shoulds* with the realities that they see? How can we help them to clarify their values so that they can make choices that are congruent with their true feelings?

The object of this chapter is to present to teachers some ideas that they can use to help students clarify their own feelings and values. Along the way, the reader may become aware of a degree of confusion in his own valuing process; but it is no more necessary that a teacher working with student values have a clearly defined value structure than it is necessary for a football coach to play all the positions better than the people on his team. Valuing is a continuing process for all of us.

THE ELEMENTS OF VALUING

In talking about values in the classroom, we have found it useful to divide the valuing process into six elements, four dealing with choosing, two with acting:[2]

CHOOSING

1. *Preferences:*   What do I really like?

2. *Influences:*   What influences have led me to this decision? How freely am I making my choice?

3. *Alternatives:*   What are the possible alternatives to this choice? Have I given sufficient consideration to such alternatives?

4. *Consequences:*   What are the probable and possible consequences for my choice?

Am I willing to risk the consequences? Are the consequences socially beneficial or socially harmful?

ACTING

5. *Acting:* Am I able to act on this choice? Do my actions reflect the choice I have made?

6. *Patterning:* Does this choice represent a continuing commitment through action? How can I change the pattern of my life so that this choice is continually reflected in my actions?

These last two elements are very important because a great deal of evidence indicates that a person's behavior does not necessarily correspond to his attitudes. It is this lack of congruence which accounts for much of the personal dissatisfaction, anxiety, and apparent apathy which are often reflected in young people's behavior.

Test, if you will, one of your values against these six elements: write down very briefly a value you have connected with leisure time. Say, for instance, that you value hiking as a part of your life. You feel that you have chosen hiking freely, over other leisure-time alternatives, and with a consideration of the consequences. You feel that hiking is one of your preferences; but when it comes to acting, you find that you have not done any hiking for more than a month, and that hiking forms no consistent pattern in your life. If you really value hiking, how must you change your life so that you can live more in accordance with your value? If you don't really value hiking, if you discover that there are other things that you value more highly, then perhaps you can feel less guilty about watching a football game on T.V. on a brilliant Sunday afternoon.

THREE STEPS FOR WORKING WITH VALUES

The first step in helping others with the valuing process is to *open* the area — to stimulate a person to think about value-related areas and to encourage him to share his thoughts with others. Perhaps the simplest way to encourage value exploration within the classroom is to stop the normal progress of the lesson when you feel that an important value area is being touched upon and to say, "Let's see how we can clarify this," or, "Let's deal with this."

The next step is to *accept* the thoughts, feelings, beliefs, and ideas of others non-judgmentally, and to encourage the others in the class to accept a person's feelings for what they are, without criticism. This step helps the individual to know that he can be honest with others and with himself, no matter how negative or confused his feelings and ideas might be. It is important always to respect a student's right to "pass," that is, to refuse to share his thoughts and feelings if he feels that the risks are too high. (Obviously, it is important to help the individual to increase his level of risk-taking, but this should not be done by attempting to force an issue.)

The third step is to *stimulate* additional thinking so that an individual can move toward a more comprehensive way of valuing. The six elements of valuing provide some of the kinds of thoughts and considerations that are helpful to an individual as he grapples with his values. What are the alternatives that you might consider? Where would this idea lead — what would the consequences be? Is this something that you have chosen freely, or is it something that you have been taught to believe?

It is important to use such clarifying questions sparingly and in a non-judgmental way. For instance, if a teacher sees a student pick up a snow ball and says, "Have you considered the consequences of that action?" it does not matter how non-judgmental the teacher feels, the student, from long experience, will infer a criticism, a put-down.

NOTE: The activities which follow deal with value judgments and other issues of concern to students, and of importance to their sense of self. Although the decisions and responses called for in these activities are of necessity personal, part of the value of the activities in promoting personal and social growth is in providing opportunities for discussion of the issues raised. Therefore, it is most important that ample time be allowed for discussion after each activity or each part of a more extended one. The expanded awareness and enhanced power of empathy which come from such discussions are vital human values.

ACTIVITIES FOR VALUE EXPLORATION

Subject: *Value Voting.*

Material: None.

Procedure:

1. With the class divided into small groups, the students vote on questions related to values. The teacher gives the following instructions: "To show agreement or positive feelings toward the question, raise your hand. If you feel very strongly in favor, wave your hand in the air. If you disagree or feel negative toward the question, turn your thumb down. For a very strong negative vote, turn your thumb down and make a churning motion. If you have no feelings or wish to pass, fold your arms across your chest."

2. The teacher then asks a series of questions which involve judgments (see below). There should be no attempt to tally the vote.

3. At the end of a few questions, there should be a break to allow the members of the groups to share their feelings. They will probably wish to explore areas of disagreement and agreement with each other.

Sample Questions

1. Would you try sky diving?

2. Would you tell someone he has bad breath?

3. Would you favor a more stringent dress code?

4. Would you like to try marijuana, at least once?

5. Do you think that the Apollo Program was a waste of our natural resources?

6. Would you carry a sign in a protest march?

7. Would you buy a vacation in Hawaii on credit?

8. Would you change your hairstyle if it meant earning 20 per cent more money?

Value voting can be useful for clarifying values in subject matter too:

History: Do you approve of John Brown's actions at Harper's Ferry?

English: Do you approve of Ma's actions in getting rid of Flag in *The Yearling?*

Science: Do you approve of vivisection?

In making up questions to vote on, the emphasis should be kept on the *you.* Action-oriented questions are good. And the questions should be taken from areas of real concern. Once they get the idea, the students will come up with relevant questions of their own. Again, it is important that everyone understand his right to pass if the questions seem too threatening.

Subject: *Rank Order.*

Material: None.

Procedure:

1. Divide into small groups. Students are given three situations to rank as they perceive them, from best to worst; if they perceive them as all good (or all bad), they are to rank from most good (bad) to least. Rankings should be made individually.

2. Compare rankings and discuss with the others in the group. (It is possible, as with any of these activities, that students will prefer to open the discussion to the class as a whole.)

Suggested situations to rank

1. You are an Air Force bombardier about to drop bombs on suspected enemy troop concentrations, knowing that innocent civilians are likely to be struck as well.

2. You must pull the switch on a convicted murderer in the electric chair.

3. You are a home-owner who is about to shoot at a dark moving shape which has entered your home at night.

After discussing your rank orders, try this one: If you were the principal of this school, rank these situations as to their desirability to you:

1. The students love you.

2.   Your colleagues respect your opinion.

3.   Your school is the showplace of the district.

After discussing your rank ordering of these situations, try to expand this list by making up a situation that would be more desirable than the one you put at the top, and one that would be less desirable than your bottom-ranked situation.

Now, assume you are the parent of a seventeen-year-old girl, and try ranking these situations.

1.   You discover that she has the reputation of being promiscuous.

2.   You receive a call from the police that she has been arrested for possession of marijuana.

3.   She announces to you that she is engaged to marry a boy of another race.

After discussing your rankings, talk about how the list might change if the seventeen-year-old had been a son instead of a daughter.

The three rank orders above all involve taking another role. To that extent, they give the individual a chance to glimpse the world from another's point of view. It is also useful to make up rank orders that involve everyday choice situations for students, such as which is best to do when you see another student copying off your paper in a test:

1.   Do nothing.

2. Hide your paper as well as you can with your arm, realizing that you cannot work as well in that position.

3. Call the teacher and ask if you can change your seat.

What other possibilities can you come up with?

A person in your class whom you don't like very well has been accused of taking some lunch money from the teacher's desk. You saw someone else take the money. How do you rank the following?

1. Take no action.

2. Defend the person openly, knowing that you will be pressured to tell who really took the money.

3. Write an anonymous letter to the principal explaining the situation without identifying the real thief.

What are some other possibilities? As with value voting, students can learn to make up rank-order situations to help clarify important issues in their own lives.

Here are some uses of rank-order problems in relation to traditional course content:

English: Rank Macbeth's motives for killing Duncan, from most powerful to least powerful:

1. To please his wife.

2. To gain power for himself.

3. To gain wealth.

4. To fulfill the prophecy of the witches.

History: Rank the following reasons that General Lee might have given for joining the Confederate Army rather than the Union Army:

1. To maintain slavery.

2. To assert the right of states to self-determination.

3. To defend his homeland.

4. To maintain his Southern life-style.

Math: Rank the following reasons for studying algebra in order of their importance to you:

1. Because it's a required course.

2. For future benefit—use in college.

3. For future benefit—use in my everyday life.

4. Training for my mind.

FORCED-CHOICE GAMES

Forced-choice games represent another type of activity designed to open the area of valuing and to stimulate additional thinking. As with any value exploration, it is important to accept the feelings of the student openly and non-judgmentally, so that he can learn to become more open and direct about his feelings without fear of reprisal or rebuke.

Almost any subject matter can be used for a forced-choice game. For younger children, for instance, you could make up a Noah's Ark game: Which five or six pairs of animals would you choose to put in the ark, and what are the characteristics of those animals that you admire? A desert island game could force a choice about characters, or electrical appliances, or five things that are in a person's room.

Subject: *Space Ambassadors.*

Material: Paper, pencils, lists of volunteers.

Procedure:

1.   After dividing the class into groups, the teacher tells the students the following: "Your group has been given the responsibility of selecting five persons from the list of volunteer candidates below who are to be sent as the first representatives from Earth to a planet in a distant galaxy which is known to contain human life. Do not worry about problems of time, space, language, or life support, for modern technology can fulfill these needs. You will have fifteen minutes to reach a group decision.

Try to avoid artificial means of decision making such as voting or flipping coins."

The volunteers are:

1. Assistant manager, New York bank, resident of Long Island, age 39.

2. His wife, 37.

3. Welfare recipient, mother of six, Puerto Rican, 32.

4. Head of local construction firm, son of Italian immigrant, 48.

5. Catholic priest, white, 28.

6. Editor of university daily newspaper, 20.

7. Army major, Vietnam veteran, 46.

8. Model for television commercials, male, 49.

9. High school dropout, working in neighborhood youth center, 18.

10. President, New England Chapter, World Federalists, female, 68.

11. Artist whose work appears in leading national magazine, involved in a group marriage, 41.

12. His younger wife, writer of unpublished children's stories, 19.

13. His older wife, M.D., just published major research on cancer, 47.

14. Chief, Black-fox tribe, Chena American Indians, 87.

15. Principal, urban elementary school, white, 43.

2. Say: "It would be nice if there were more data available on these candidates, but you must remember that in the real world we are continually forced to make judgments based upon incomplete data.

"After your committee has reached its decision, discuss what values you hope the chosen five will communicate."

Subject: *Value Whips.*

Material: None.

Procedure: This activity consists of having each person in turn share his feelings and ideas about a given topic: for instance, "The time I felt closest to nature this week was . . ." or "The high point of my week was. . . ." As the whip moves from person to person around the room, there is often a growing awareness of the commonality of man, as well as of the varieties of experience. Sometimes a whip can give a person new ideas about how he can change his life or add new skills to his repertoire. As each student examines himself and articulates his feelings, he comes to know himself better, and to begin to know and value his feelings for what they are. If a whip topic touches too closely upon a person's life, and if he is not prepared to move to that level of risk-taking, he can pass. The teacher should not be afraid to include himself in the whip.

Here are some possible whips:

> "The thing that disturbed me most this week was . . ."

> "The time I had the most fun with children this week was . . ."

> "The time I had the most fun with adults this week was . . ."

> "I wonder . . ."

> "The new skill I learned this summer that I am proud of is . . ."

> "I am proud that I have helped race relations by . . ."

> "I am proud that I struck a blow against pollution by . . ."

> "I wish . . ."

A whip is a good way to start a class, or to end a class. It lets the students know that their feelings are important and that it is proper to deal with their feelings in the classroom.

Subject: *Value Cards.*

Material: 3 x 5 cards, pencils.

Procedure:

1. Ask the students to bring in a 3 x 5 card once a week on which they have composed a statement about what they value. The card can be prose or a poem, or a picture, or a collage, any statement of value to the person.

2. The card is not to be graded in any way, but the teacher will read two or three cards each day, anonymously unless the author wishes to reveal himself. On some days the class can be asked to comment, on others not.

3. At the end of the term, the cards can be passed back to the students so that they can see how they have progressed in valuing.

Subject: *"I Learned . . ." Statements.*

Material: None.

Procedure: At the end of a discussion about values, after one of the other activities (for the use of "I Learned . . ." Statements in information processing, see page 143), it can be clarifying to ask for some "I Learned . . ." Statements. It is generally better not to use a whip for "I Learned . . ." Statements but to let anyone who wants to share speak out. Every "I Learned . . ." Statement should have two I's: "I learned that I . . .''; "I re-learned that I . . ."; "I noticed that I . . ."; "I re-affirmed that I . . . ." It is important to keep the focus on what a person has learned about himself. Some "I learned [about something] " Statements will slip by, but the closer the group can be kept to the second I, the more each participant will learn about his own feelings and values. For example, if a student says, "I learned that all people are different," it is probably not as helpful to him as if he had said, "I learned that I often forget how different people are."

ACTIVITIES FOR IDENTIFYING STUDENT CONCERNS

A teacher who is committed to promulgating human values in the classroom must help students to identify not only their values, but also their concerns. Indeed, Neil Postman and Charles Weingartner tell us, in *Teaching as a Subversive Activity,* that we must build the curriculum around the student concerns. But what *are* student concerns? This is a difficult question for students to answer directly, and a more difficult question for teachers to deal with. Here is a variety of activities which are designed to identify the concerns of students, what things they view as important.

Subject: *Areas of Concern Questionnaire.*

Material: *Areas of Concern Questionnaires* (see page 163), pencils.

Procedure:

1. The teacher passes out two copies of the *Questionnaire* to each student and asks the students to mark one copy "Private" and the other "Public."

2. The student fills out the "Public" *Questionnaire* by writing one question below each of the areas of concern listed, omitting any area that is not a matter of concern to the student.

3. While the students are working on the "Public" *Questionnaire*, they may use the "Private" *Questionnaire* to write down questions that come to them on any area of concern, questions which they feel are too personal or risky to share. No one will ask to see the "Private" *Questionnaire*—its purpose is to help students define personal problems for themselves.

4. After the students have filled out the *Questionnaires* (allow about five minutes), the class is divided into small groups of five or six. Each group selects one concern from the list, and each group member reads his question relating to that concern.

5. The group brainstorms on either one of the following topics: additional questions about that area of concern, or sub-questions of one of the student's questions.

6. This can be followed by having each group choose a second area of concern to work on, or by having each

student read his entire list of concerns to the group. Or, the exercise can be finished by having each group report to the entire class.

7.   The teacher should collect the "Public" *Questionnaires* as a valuable source of insight into student concerns.

Areas of Concern Questionnaire

Directions: Write one question concerning each of the following topics in the space below that topic. Omit any topic which is not a concern of yours, and add any topic or topics that do concern you.

_____

PUBLIC OR PRIVATE

1.   Friendship

2.   Love

3.   Family

4.   Self-appraisal

5.   Sex

6.   Time

7.   Politics

8. Race

9. Leisure

10. Commitment

11. Work

12. Religion

13. Money

14. Drugs

15. War

16. Intimacy

17. Communication

18. Education

19. Authority

20. Beauty

21. The future

22.

23.

Subject: *Future Questions.*

Material: Chalkboard, paper, pencils.

Procedure:

1. For four minutes, the class brainstorms questions that they have about the future, questions that will probably be answered in one or two years. The questions are recorded on the blackboard.

2. Next, the class brainstorms for four minutes questions about the future that probably won't be answered in one or two years. A separate section of the board is used to record these questions.

3. Students are asked to brainstorm by themselves silently, thinking of questions about their own personal futures, and writing them down. This last list is private writing — the students will not be forced to share their personal future questions with anyone.

4. After four minutes of private brainstorming, the teacher asks the class to look over the three lists — their personal lists and the two on the board — and to pick five questions concerning the future that they feel are most important to them. These five questions are to be rank ordered.

5. The students are divided into small groups and directed to share as many of the five questions as they wish,

noting similarities and differences.

6. Remaining in small groups, the students may work on one or more of the questions, brainstorming ways that they can act in order to affect the answer to a "future question."

Subject: *Current Events.*

Material: Chalkboard, pencils, paper.

Procedure:

1. The teacher asks the class to brainstorm important events that have taken place during the last year. These are recorded on the blackboard for all to see, and the brainstorming is halted once fifteen items have been recorded. Each student writes down one additional current event which is not on the list but should be.

2. The teacher asks the students to divide a piece of paper into four columns of four boxes each, and to label the first column "Most Important"; the second column, "Important"; the third, "Less Important"; and the fourth, "Least Important." Then the boxes are numbered from one to sixteen, as in the diagram below.

3. Students are to fill in each block, ranking the current events in order of importance to themselves.

4. The papers are then folded so that only the first column appears. The students form into small groups, and compare their rankings of the first column. Each group may be asked to report its findings to the class, noting agreements and disagreements, and patterns where they occur.

MOST IMPORTANT	IMPORTANT	LESS IMPORTANT	LEAST IMPORTANT
1	5	9	13
2	6	10	14
3	7	11	15
4	8	12	16

Subject: *I Am the Picture.*[3]

Material: *"I Am the Picture" Worksheets* (see page 169), ambiguous pictures (see description below), pencils or pens.

Procedure:

1. The teacher divides the class into small groups, and posts a picture containing one or two figures. The picture may be taken from a newspaper or magazine, or it may be a photograph, drawing, or painting. If the picture is too

small for the entire class to see well, the teacher may use several different pictures, one for each group. The picture should involve a situation which is in some way ambiguous.

2. The students are asked to concentrate on one of the figures in the picture for one minute, noticing any clues in terms of clothes, facial expression, body language, and surrounding objects. Then the teacher asks the students to imagine that they *are* the figure.

3. After a few moments, the teacher passes out the *"I Am the Picture"* Worksheets and asks the students to complete the sentence stems.

4. The sentences are shared in small groups. The teacher may call for a group report in which the students focus on the variety of interpretations within the group.

5. As an alternative to the sentence-stem completions, or in addition to it, the teacher can ask each student to write a story of five or six sentences about the figure, writing as though the student were the figure. The stories then can be shared and/or posted on the wall, or made into a book with the picture bound in.

"I Am the Picture" Worksheet

1. I've just come from . . .

2. Now I'm thinking about . . .

3. One thing that I'm afraid of is . . .

4. What I'd like most to do now is . . .

5. One question that I have is . . .

6. I'm happiest when . . .

7. I feel most important when . . .

8. I'm saddest when . . .

9. If I could have one wish, it would be . . .

10. I like to be called . . .

Subject: *Coping Questions.*

Material: "Coping Questions Box" (just like a suggestions box).

Procedure:

1. The teacher introduces the idea of "coping questions" by pointing out that we all have minor problems in coping with the hustle and bustle of everyday life, and that finding out how others handle certain situations may help us cope with similar problems. For example: How do you decide when not to watch TV? How do you handle all the homework that you're supposed to do? How do you handle money — do you spend it carefully, considering options and taking a lot of time before making a choice (and sometimes wasting time because of that), or do you go out on a spree every now and then? How do you plan for your vacations? How do you make sure you get enough sleep? And so on. The teacher will get the best response to the notion of coping questions if he uses real questions from his own life as examples for initial discussion.

2. For each of the questions that the teacher raises, he allows a brief period for comment, focusing on alternative methods of coping with the problems as practiced by the members of the class. The floor is then thrown open for anyone who has a coping question to pose to the group.

3. On short notice, the class may not come up with questions of their own; however, the teacher can announce that there will be a "coping question" period once or twice a week, and urge students to place questions that they might like to discuss in the "Coping

Questions Box." The papers need not be signed. It is advisable to remind students of the Coping Question Box on the day before the coping question period, possibly allowing some class time for individual reflection and the formation of questions for the box.

Subject: *Decisions — An Open-Chair Brainstorm and Role Play.*

Material: Two extra chairs, two pieces of paper with circle faces drawn on, tape, two pieces of paper labeled "Temporary Member."

Procedure:

1. The classroom is arranged in a circle. The two open chairs are placed near the center, facing each other. The teacher designates one chair by a boy's name and the other chair by a girl's name. (Neither should be the name of a member of the class or of a person of notoriety in the school.)

2. The boys group around the boy chair and the girls group around the girl chair. If numbers are highly uneven, this sex difference need not be observed, and half of the class may be grouped around each chair.

3. The group around the boy's chair brainstorms for five minutes all the decisions that a boy their age (as represented by the chair) might have to make during

the next year of his life. The group around the girl's chair brainstorms decisions that a girl their age (as represented by the girl chair) might have to make during the next year.

4.   After the brainstorming, the girl's list is read aloud to the whole class. The boy's group should listen very carefully so that they may add any idea that the girl's group missed. After the list has been read, any immediate suggestions for additional decisions are solicited from the boy's group and these are added to the girl's list. (This is not brainstorming — only those ideas that are presented immediately should be noted.) This process is repeated for the boy's list, with the girl's group being asked to make additions.

5.   Now each group is asked to choose a decision of particular interest to that group. If the decision chosen is too general, a few minutes can· be taken to brainstorm more specific sub-decisions from the original one. At this point, there can be a general discussion of the nature of the decision to be made, what kind of additional information may be helpful in making the decision, and how to obtain additional information.

6.   Using the chosen decision, each group sets forth a situation where the decision is about to be confronted by two people (e.g., the boy has decided to drop out of school — he is about to tell his father). Or, the situation may involve a decision confrontation by two alter egos within one person (e.g., the girl is deciding whether to

spend the weekend with her boy friend and thereby lose her virginity — the two roles are her own self arguing for and against).

7. The situations are role played one at a time in the following manner: Three volunteers are chosen to play each role. They group themselves on the floor around the chair that represents the role they are playing. They face the other chair and the three other volunteers. The remainder of the class sits in chairs in one large circle around the two groups. A piece of paper marked "Temporary Member" is placed on the floor next to each group of volunteers (see diagram on page 175).

8. Now the role play begins, with one of the teams initiating the confrontation with the other team. Any member of a team may speak out as the voice of the "chair" and may be answered by any member of the opposite team. When there is indecision about what kind of response to make, the team may discuss their response among themselves before replying. This discussion should be open and loud so that all can hear. At any time, a member of the outside circle may come and sit on one of the "Temporary Member" papers and become a member of the team. No Temporary Member may stay on the team for more than three exchanges.

9. The role play should be strictly limited to ten minutes. If it has become unproductive, the role play may be terminated at the end of seven minutes. A role play should be cut when the second-hand sweeps past the

twelve, stopping the role players in mid-sentence if necessary.

10.   Each role play is followed by a discussion of the issues raised, focusing on: what factors affect the decision; what additional information would be helpful in making the decision; what are possible alternative courses of action; what consequences are likely to result from the decision; and how to obtain help and guidance in making this kind of decision.

NOTE: The open chair is used to reduce the level of risk in surfacing real concerns of students. Because it is the concern of "a boy their age" or "a girl their age," individual students do not have to "own" the concern. The use of teams to play each role reduces the threat of one individual being identified with the decisions which the role character is making. The "Temporary Member" place is used to keep the interest and involvement of the outside circle. Strict timing relieves the role players of the burden of trying to structure some kind of conclusion to the drama, a burden which generally diminishes the vitality and authenticity of the role play. Finally, the position of the teacher emphasizes the neutrality of his role.

Class Arrangement for *Open-Chair Role Play*

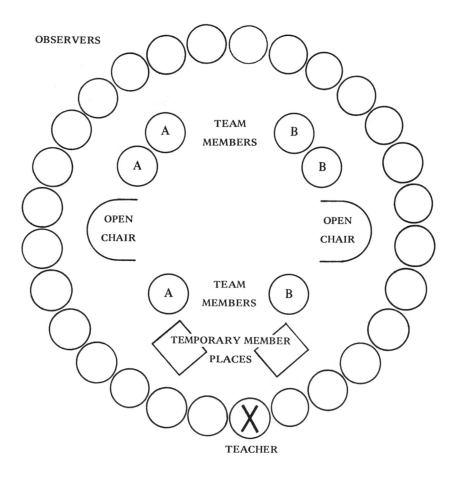

OBSERVERS

A A   TEAM MEMBERS   B B

OPEN CHAIR   OPEN CHAIR

A   TEAM MEMBERS   B

TEMPORARY MEMBER PLACES

TEACHER

Subject: *Group Dreams — Round Robin.*

Material: Paper, pencil (or tape recorder).

Procedure:

1. The class is divided into groups of seven to ten students. Each group arranges itself in a circle. A piece of paper with a circle face is placed on the floor in the center of each group.

2. The group invents a dream for the "person" in the center of the circle, using the following procedure: The students talk as though they are the person and the dream is happening right now. One student starts the dream by closing his eyes and saying, "I see . . ." and then completing the sentence as the dreamer might, inventing the beginning of the dream. Then going around the circle to the right, each student in turn closes his eyes and adds one idea to the dream, starting with "Now I see . . ." or "Now I hear . . ." or "Now I feel . . ." or "Now I sense . . ." and then completing the sentence. One person in the group is designated as the recorder, or the dream can be tape recorded for later replay.

3. After the dream, students discuss what major concerns seemed to be raised through the dream.

NOTE: Direct or symbolic analysis of the dream is to be strongly discouraged, as this generally leads to vapid intellectualizing. "Lloyd's of London — Specialized Insurance" (see below) is a useful follow-up to this exercise.

Subject: *Lloyd's of London — Specialized Insurance Policies.*

Material: Chalkboard, pencils, paper.

Procedure:

1. The teacher introduces the concept of insurance policies for life, accident, fire, theft, etc. He notes that none of these policies actually prevents the *occurrence* of the disaster insured against, but merely offers money payments to counterbalance the disaster when (or if) it occurs. A good illustration of this point is the well-known story about the first life-insurance salesman to visit the Fiji Islands. He was pleased and surprised at the number of life insurance policies that he sold. On returning to the Islands some weeks later, however, he was greeted with irate hostility and informed in no uncertain terms that his life insurance was no good — someone had died.

2. The teacher asks the students to focus on the positive side of insurance policies. For instance, instead of taking out a policy against rain for the day of the class picnic, there could be a policy that would provide for bright sunshine and temperatures in the mid-seventies for that day. Instead of a policy against failing the final exam for

a course, there might be a policy to insure at least an 87 on it. Students then brainstorm for five minutes on special insurance policies that they would like to see available.

3. After the general brainstorming, the class divides into small groups, each choosing one policy to work on. For three minutes, they brainstorm special conditions that could enhance their policy. (For instance, on the Eternal Life Policy, special conditions might include eternal youth, vigor, wisdom, sex appeal, etc. For the Most Beautiful Home Policy, special conditions might include a garden with continuously blooming flowers, heated outdoor swimming pool, no maintenance, congenial neighbors, etc.)

4. After the special-conditions brainstorm, the group goes back to its original policy and brainstorms ways that this policy can be most nearly implemented. (For example, the Eternal Life Policy can be most nearly implemented by getting enough rest, exercising, eating the right foods, driving carefully, etc.)

5. Finally, the teacher asks each student to reflect on one thing that he might do that will help to implement his own special insurance policy.

Subject: *Pockets.*

Material: Chalkboard (pencils, paper).

Procedure:

1. The teacher points out to the class that one way to identify the concerns and interests of younger students is to ask them to empty their pockets. Out will come hot-wheel cars, marbles, plastic monsters, yo-yos, keys, pennies, football player cards, etc. While older students are not so likely to carry bulgy stuff around in their pockets, they do have certain repositories for objects which show their interests and concerns. No, no one will have to empty his wallet or her pocketbook out in front of the class; no one will be forced to bring in the contents of his top bureau drawer, but it might prove useful to identify some of the "pockets" which older students have, and to give students opportunities to catalogue the "stuff" in those pockets. This procedure may help students to be more aware of their own interests.

2. By sharing the lists, or as much of their lists as individuals are willing to share, students may find which interests and concerns are common and which are unique.

3. The class may proceed by brainstorming some of the "pockets" for meaningful objects, and then brainstorm what kinds of things are likely to be in those pockets.

4. The teacher then encourages the students to look through some of their "pockets" at home and to catalogue the items in one of these "pockets" that they

would be willing to let the others in the class know about. The next day, these catalogues can be shared in small groups or by bulletin-board displays.

Subject: *The Marijuana Story.*[4]

Material: *The Marijuana Story* (see below), pencils and paper.

Procedure:

1.   The teacher reads or tells "The Marijuana Story."

The Marijuana Story

Tim, a high school student, moves with his parents to a new community in October of his senior year. He is rather shy and doesn't make friends easily; most of his fellow students regard him as a "brain" because he is taking accelerated courses in science and math. His parents want him to go to college and have decided that he is not to go out on school nights; he must stay home and study.

Pam is in Tim's American History class. She thinks he's cute and has been trying to coax him into asking her out for a date. Tim, however, has never considered this because Pam is a cheerleader and a member of the popular set at school, and anyhow, Tim has to stay in and study most of the time.

One Tuesday afternoon, Pam gives in to impatience and asks Tim over for the evening to listen to records. Tim eagerly accepts. At dinner that night he tells his parents that he is going over to a friend's house to work on a science project and will be home around ten o'clock. At seven he makes his escape.

He goes to Pam's house and soon they are in the cellar recreation room talking and listening to the stereo. About eight o'clock, Pam reaches into her pocket and pulls out a plastic bag. She asks Tim if he'd like to smoke some grass. Tim takes the bag and looks inside it. He is curious about marijuana — he has never seen it before.

Suddenly Pam's father walks in. He halts and stares at the couple and then grabs the bag from Tim. He looks at Tim and then at his daughter. "Is this marijuana?" he inquires. Pam looks down, and Tim sits there, speechless. "Pam," says her father, "You go to your room while I take this young hood to the police station.

"What's your name, boy?"

Tim is scared. He blurts out the name of one of the kids in his class rumored to sell drugs.

Pam's father leads Tim to the car muttering imprecations about slum punks and bad apples that ruin the whole barrel. Once in the car, he calms down and asks Tim where he lives. Tim tells him his address, hoping he won't be taken to the police station.

Finally, they arrive at Tim's house, and in the heat of Pam's father's confrontation with Tim's parents, no introductions take place. Pam's father departs shortly saying, "The only reason I brought him home is that I don't want to put a kid in jail just because he's had the misfortune of a bad upbringing."

Tim's mother starts on a rampage of verbal abuse. "How long has this been going on? After all I've done for you; now you slap me in the face. We gave you everything!" His father motions him to go to his room and says, "Get some sleep. We'll talk about this in the morning when we've all calmed down."

In the morning, Tim finds that his father has gone to work early and his mother has some news for him: "Your father and I had a long talk last night and I finally persuaded him to go along with my decision. From now on you'll do *all* of your studying at home. Weekends you'll work in your father's store and all of your earnings will be put away for your college education."

2. The students are told to rank the characters in order, from the one whose actions they most approve to the one whose actions they least approve: Tim, Pam, Pam's father, Tim's father, Tim's mother.

Possible follow-up activities:

1. Students can divide into small groups and share and discuss their rank orders. The teacher can ask for a show of hands, "How many ranked Tim as the one whose actions you most approved of? How many ranked Pam there?" Etc.

2. Five areas in the room are designated by the names of the characters (Tim in the left-hand corner by the window, Pam in the right-hand corner, etc.). Students are asked to move to the area which represents their highest-ranked character. The groups that meet in each

area discuss their reasons and share them informally with the entire class (Teacher might say, "Is there a spokesman for Tim's corner?" Etc.). Then this procedure can be repeated for the character at the bottom of the rank order.

3. The ideas generated by the story and the rank ordering of characters can be further explored through role playing.
    a. What should Pam's father have done when he saw the marijuana? Role play that situation.
    b. What should Tim's mother have done after Pam's father left the house? Role play that situation.
    c. What should Tim do now? Role play the morning meeting with his mother.

A whole new round of reflection and discussion can be stimulated by asking the following: Would you feel different about the story if the marijuana had been LSD? Would that change your rankings?

Any of these activities can be followed by asking students to write an "I believe . . ." or "I learned . . ." Statement in their notebooks.

ACTIVITIES FOR FORMING IDENTITY

Ask a young person, "Who are you?" Chances are he'll give you his name. Keep at it; ask him to tell you ten persons he is. He will probably say that he is, for example, a student, a basketball player, son of Mr. and Mrs. Doe, brother of Johnny, someone who got an 84 on his bio exam. And he probably won't reach ten.

We tend to think of ourselves in terms of our activities (a basketball player), our relationships (brother of Johnny), and our achievements (an 84-getter). But what we feel, what we value, what concerns us — these important considerations are rarely taken into account when we try to answer the question "Who Am I?"

The activities in this section are designed to give special insight into that question. The teacher should be sure to remind the students to keep a steady positive focus when they examine themselves. Given a page of positive feedback and a page of negative feedback, many students will believe only the negative, ultimately remember only the negative. Positive focus is not an artificial attempt to bolster weak egos — it is an effort to counter the powerful cultural forces which lead us to focus so heavily on our shortcomings.

Subject: *How Do You Feel Today?*

Material: *How Do You Feel Today? Worksheets* (see page 185), pencils or pens.

Procedure:

1.   The teacher distributes the worksheets and allows students three or four minutes to fill them in. This is

private writing: no one will be forced to share his paper with anyone else.

2. Groups of three or four are formed to discuss the activity, sharing any of the items on the worksheet that they care to. "I Learned . . ." Statements can be called for at this time.

How Do You Feel Today?

Directions: Circle the number on each continuum that is closest to the way you feel right now.

1	2	3	4	5	6	7
Unfulfilled						Satisfied

1	2	3	4	5	6	7
Supported						Rejected

1	2	3	4	5	6	7
Confused						Clear

1	2	3	4	5	6	7
Shy						Curious

1	2	3	4	5	6	7
Involved						Bored

1	2	3	4	5	6	7
Frustrated						Contented

1	2	3	4	5	6	7
Superior						Inferior

1	2	3	4	5	6	7
Suspicious						Trusting

1	2	3	4	5	6	7
Fulfilled						Empty

1	2	3	4	5	6	7
Hurt						Relieved

1	2	3	4	5	6	7
Friendly						Lonely

1	2	3	4	5	6	7
Loving						Hating

1	2	3	4	5	6	7
Joyful						Sad

1	2	3	4	5	6	7
Angry						Affectionate

1	2	3	4	5	6	7
Hopeful						Fearful

1	2	3	4	5	6	7
Strong						Weak

Pick one or two feelings that you wish to change and brainstorm things that you can do to effect that change. Then, select one or two ideas from your brainstorm list, refine the ideas if necessary, and contract with yourself to do what the idea calls for.

Subject: *Here-and-Now Words.*

Material: Pencils, paper.

Procedure:

1. The teacher instructs the students as follows: "Write the date and the exact time, and then write four words or brief phrases that describe feelings you have right here and now. Then take one of those four items and write two sentences expanding on that feeling."

   Here-and-now words are an attempt to get in touch with what is really going on inside the self. If and when a class develops the openness and the positiveness and the ability to give non-judgmental feedback, the sharing of here-and-now words can be a significant clarifying technique.

2. In addition to the immediate self-awareness that here-and-now words can bring, an individual can gain insight into his patterns of feelings and behaviors by comparing here-and-now words collected over a period of time and from different situations. The teacher might, for in-

stance, ask each member of a class to write here-and-now words at a given time each day for two weeks, or once a week for a term, or each waking hour for one day, and then to assemble his here-and-now words and see what patterns of feeling run through the current of his life.

Subject: *Who Am I?*[5]

Material: 3 x 5 cards, or used computer cards, or recycled paper cut into approximately three-inch squares — ten pieces for each student; pencils or pens.

Procedure:

1.   Each student receives ten cards. The teacher asks the class to write an answer to the question, "Who am I?" on each of the ten cards.

2.   After the students have identified themselves in ten different ways on the cards, the teacher asks them to arrange the cards in order of importance to them, with the most important card on top and the least important card on the bottom. The students should write down the order in their notebooks so that they will have a permanent record. Then the teacher asks the students to turn their piles over so that the least important card is on top and the cards are face down.

3.   The teacher instructs the students to pick up the card

which is on top, read it, and then tear it up and throw it on the floor. (If the cards are later to be used for the "Who Am I? — Who Do You Think I Am?" activity which follows, the cards are merely dropped on the floor without being torn up.) The teacher repeats the instruction to pick up the top card, read it, and then destroy it until all ten cards have been destroyed. Occasionally as a card has been destroyed, the teacher may ask a process question such as, "Are you glad or sorry that that one is gone?" "Are you still happy about the order that you placed the cards in?" "Are there any cards that should have been ranked higher?" "Can you think of both good and bad things about having that card go?" Spontaneous comments from students during this process should be welcomed and encouraged — "How are you feeling now?" It is particularly important here to keep the atmosphere scrupulously non-judgmental.

4. When only one card remains, the teacher may ask, "How do you feel now with only one card left? Can you think of any other card that you would rather have now, or would you like to make a new card at this point, one that you didn't think of before?"

5. After all the cards have been dropped, the teacher may ask for each student to write one or two "I Learned . . ." Statements in his notebook. Afterwards, there can be a period when anyone who wishes to can share his "I Learned . . ." Statement with the class.

6. After the sharing of "I Learned . . ." Statements, the

teacher may ask the students to pick up only those cards that they want back.

7. By show of hands, the teacher may poll how many wanted all their cards back, how many wanted all but one; but two; how many left more than two cards on the floor.

Subject: *Who Am I? — Who Do You Think I Am?*

Material: Same as "Who Am I?" above.

Procedure:

1. This is an extension of the "Who Am I?" activity. The teacher asks the students to collect their ten cards, form pairs, shuffle their own cards, and exchange them with the other member of the pair.

2. Individuals arrange the cards in rank order, trying to guess how their partners ranked them. This extension gives students a chance to practice empathizing, and also gives valuable feedback on the question, "How am I perceived by others?"

Subject: *To Tell the Truth.*

Material: *Master of Ceremonies Instruction Sheets* (see page 192), pencils and paper.

Procedure:

1. Each student writes a paragraph of six or seven sentences describing an exciting incident from his life.

2. Groups of seven or nine are formed; one person from each group is designated as master of ceremonies; and the rest are divided into subgroups of three or four. Each subgroup plans separately and secretly for seven minutes, deciding which of their three stories to use for the game and what strategies they may use to fool the "panel of experts" (one of the subgroups will be "experts," the other will be "guests").

3. Meanwhile, the master of ceremonies from each group meets with the teacher to go over the *Master of Ceremonies Instruction Sheet.* Then each M.C. goes to both of his own subgroups to pick up the story each has chosen and rehearses his reading silently.

4. When the planning period has ended, the subgroups reunite, one becoming the panel of experts, the other the mystery guests. The master of ceremonies reads the story, and then each member of the panel in turn asks three questions.

5. After three rounds of questioning, the panel votes on who is the real author of the story. Then the master of ceremonies asks the real author to please stand up.

6. The panel and the mystery guests then switch roles and the game is replayed.

7. After this second round, the master of ceremonies asks each of the other players to read his own story to the group, and the master of ceremonies reads his own story to the group.

8. "To Tell the Truth" can also be played by the whole class together, with the teacher acting as master of ceremonies.

Master of Ceremonies Instruction Sheet

1. Pick up the chosen story from each of your subgroups and read it over carefully, and rehearse it if you wish so that you can read it aloud later without revealing the author's identity.

2. When your two subgroups return, flip a coin to see which will be the mystery guests first. Then set up your group in two semi-circles with the guests facing the panel.

3. Read the mystery guests' story, and then ask the panel to start the questioning.

4. Allow each panel member to ask three questions at a turn (or one question to each of the three mystery guests), and then move on to the next member.

5. Keep track of the questions to be sure that each panel member gets three turns but no more. If the panel members have trouble thinking of questions, you can suggest using one of these for a starter:

"How did it feel when . . . ?"

"What were you thinking when . . . ?"

"What did your mother do when . . . ?"

6. When all members of the panel have had three turns, give the panel members one minute to write down their votes for the real author of the story. Then ask each to tell his guess.

7. As each person makes his guess, try to get him to give his reasons for his decision. See if you can get him to be as specific as possible.

8. Keep track of the score, but don't overplay the aspect of competition; the game is to be played for fun.

9. After both subgroups have had a turn as panel and mystery guests, let everyone whose story was not read have a chance to share his story with the group. Anyone may pass, of course, but encourage all to share.

Subject: *Life Auction.*[6]

Material: *Life Auction Catalogue Sheets* (see page 196); play money, poker chips, or used computer cards — twenty per person; pencils.

Procedure:

1. The teacher distributes the *Life Auction Catalogue Sheets* and asks the students to select four or five items that are very important to them, and to rank order those items from most to least important.

2. The teacher asks students to reflect for a few moments and to try to write in the blank spaces one or two items which are also very important.

3. The class is divided into groups of three or four, and students are asked to share their lists. For four or five minutes, they discuss what are the really important things in life.

4. Now the auction begins. The money is distributed, each member of the class getting twenty pieces, each representing $1,000. Bids must be raised by a minimum of $1,000. One student is appointed banker to collect the money during the auction. Then the teacher auctions off the list, writing down the name of the high bidder and the winning bid for each item on the board. This auction should go at a brisk pace, forcing on-the-spot decisions. After fifteen or sixteen items have been auctioned, the

teacher might ask for a show of hands on "Who hasn't bought anything yet?" and "Who has more than one item already?"

5. At the end of the auction, the teacher asks again for a show of hands from those who did not get to buy anything at the auction. He may ask them to reflect for a moment on those items that they might have bid higher for. Then the teacher tells them that if they wish, they may purchase the items that they have written in the blank spaces with their remaining money, asking each individual to assess the worth of his hand-written items in comparison to the price fetched by each item from the main list.

6. The teacher may then ask the students to write one or two "I learned . . ." Statements from this experience, or he may call for a general discussion of the activity.

NOTE: Teachers raising issues of social class, equality, and privilege in society may wish to vary the procedure by distributing the money in the following manner: Every student gets $10,000 to start with. Then each student rolls the dice to determine how many more thousands of dollars he gets (one dot equals $1,000). Those who roll a seven or more on their first roll are entitled to roll one extra die as an inheritance. Money levels may range from $12,000 to $28,000, and the questions raised concerning equality and privilege should be discussed along with the other issues.

Life Auction Catalogue Sheet

YOUR RANK ORDER	ITEM
	1. Production of a worthy off-spring.
	2. Active and satisfying sex life.
	3. Ability to influence others.
	4. Ability to draw love from others.
	5. Power over things (fix cars, program computers, build boats, etc.).
	6. Artistic ability.
	7. Active and satisfying athletic life.
	8. Opportunities for risk and adventure.
	9. Intellectual ability.
	10. Good health.
	11. Vast wealth.
	12. Approval of the opposite sex.
	13. Intellectual stimulation.
	14. Physical attractiveness.

15. Prestige.

16. Ability to initiate and maintain friendships.

17. Resilience. (Ability to bounce back.)

18. Ability to give love.

19. Socially significant activity.

20. Close and supportive family life.

21. _____

22. _____

23. _____

24. _____

25. _____

Subject: *Twenty Things I Love to Do.*[7]

Material: *Twenty-Things-I-Love-to-Do Sheets* (see page 199), pencils.

Note: This is a personal inventory which may be familiar to many, but it is included here because the authors have found it to be tremendously valuable, especially when repeated three or four times during the year. If students will date and save their sheets, further valuable insights can be gained by comparing the three or four sheets at the end of a year's time.

Procedure:

1.   The teacher hands out the *Twenty-Things-I-Love-to-Do Sheets* and asks students to fill in quickly as many such things as they can think of. Students should try to get twenty; more is all right. This is private writing. Students will not be forced to share their lists with anyone.

2.   When the students have completed their lists, the teacher asks that they search for patterns by coding their lists in the following way: In the first column, write *A* if you prefer to do the activity alone, *O* if you prefer to do it with others. In the second column, write *$* for each item that costs more than five dollars a time or that requires a significant initial investment (such as equipment). In the third column, write a minus sign (-) for any item that you expect to be missing from your list five years from now. In the fourth column, write *P* for each item that you think would occur in one of your parents' lists. In the fifth column, check each item that you have done within the last week. Finally, circle any item which you have not done within the last year.

3.   The teacher then may call for some "I Learned . . ." Statements to be written at the bottom of the page. The activity should be followed by discussion among the entire class. Anyone who wishes to share "I Learned . . ." Statements should be encouraged to do so.

Twenty-Things-I-Love-to-Do Sheet

THINGS I LOVE TO DO:	A/O	$	(-)	P	WEEK
1.					
2.					
3.					
4.					
5.					
6.					
7.					
8.					
9.					
10.					
11.					
12.					
13.					
14.					
15.					
16.					
17.					
18.					
19.					
20.					

"I learned that I . . ." _____

_____

"I discovered that I . . ." _____

_____

Subject: *Alter Ego.*[8]

Material: *Alter Ego Profile Sheets* (see page 201), pencils or pens.

Procedure:

1. Each student fills out his own *Alter Ego Profile Sheet* in response to the following:

    "If you were your alter ego, your free spirit, your other self, where would you live, what would be your choice of occupations, your hobbies, your daily bread, your choices in magazines, books, records, and entertainment. What kind of clothes would you wear and what kind of residence would you live in? Remember that your alter ego is free from all of your responsibilities, duties, and relationships. A list of close friends for your alter ego can include the names of several famous people, living, dead, or fictional."

2. After the *Profile Sheets* have been filled out, the activity can be discussed in small groups, or the following

procedure can be used: The class is divided into groups of seven. One student from each group is chosen to be the leader. The leader collects the *Alter Ego Profile Sheets* from the members of his group, including his own *Sheet.* He shuffles them and then reads each one anonymously. After each reading, members of the group try to guess the author of that *Alter Ego Profile.*

Alter Ego Profile Sheet

Directions: If you were your *alter ego,* your other self, your free spirit, freed from all your present responsibilities, duties, and relationships, what would you be like? Fill in this profile sheet and see.

1.   Where would you live?

2.   What would be your occupation?

3.   List three hobbies you might like to pursue.

4.   What foods would be on your weekly menu?

5.   List three magazines that that you would like to read.

6. What three books would probably be on your bedside table?

7. List three records, performers, or composers that would surely be among your record collection.

8. What kind of clothes would you wear —
   for dress occasions?

   for casual wear?

9. Describe your home —
   outside.

   inside.

10. If you wish, describe the sort of person you would choose to marry. You may also list your closest friends, including the names of several famous people, living, dead, or fictional.

Subject: *Adjective Rating List.*

Material: *Adjective Rating Lists* (see page 203), pencils.

Procedure:

1. Each student rates himself from one to six on each adjective, following the directions on the sheet and recording his response in the left-hand column. Then students are instructed to fold down the left-hand column so that it cannot be seen, pair with another person, and trade papers with that person. Each student fills in the column to the right on their partner's sheet, guessing for each adjective how the partner rated himself.

2. After the second rating is completed, the papers are handed back and the two columns are compared. Pairs discuss the activity; then, the entire class can comment.

NOTE: This activity gives students an opportunity to practice empathizing with another person and provides direct feedback on their ability to empathize. The activity also gives students a chance to see what sort of image they project to the world.

Adjective Rating List

Directions: This activity consists of fourteen adjectives. For each adjective mark the blank to the left of the adjective under "self":

(1)   if the adjective *almost always* describes you.

(2)   if the adjective *very often* describes you.

(3)   if the adjective *often* describes you.

(4)   if the adjective *occasionally* describes you.

(5)   if the adjective *seldom* describes you.

(6)   if the adjective *almost never* describes you.

SELF:		OTHER:
_____	1. Friendly	_____
_____	2. Aggressive	_____
_____	3. Cautious	_____
_____	4. Self-centered . . .	_____
_____	5. Confident	_____
_____	6. Apathetic	_____
_____	7. Conscientious . . .	_____
_____	8. Submissive	_____
_____	9. Adventurous	_____
_____	10. Bored	_____
_____	11. Dependable	_____
_____	12. Shy	_____
_____	13. Efficient	_____
_____	14. Enthusiastic	_____

Now pair with another person. Fold the "self" column back so that it can't be seen, and trade papers. Guess how your partner rated himself for each adjective. Record your guesses in the column to the right of the adjective under "other." After both have finished, compare the guesses with self-ratings.

Notes

1. This chapter is adapted from an article entitled "Values in the Classroom" which appeared in the *Independent School Bulletin*, October 1972.

2. This is an adaptation by Robert C. Hawley and David D. Britton of the seven valuing criteria presented in Louis E. Raths, Merrill Harmin, and Sidney B. Simon, *Values and Teaching: Working with Values in the Classroom* (Columbus, Ohio: Charles E. Merrill, 1966).

3. The originator is Norman Najimy.

4. The originator is Tom Vanderbeck.

5. The originator is Cher Stone.

6. The originator is Virginia Allison.

7. The originator is Sidney B. Simon.

8. The originator is Tom Vanderbeck.

Chapter Nine

PLANNING
FOR CHANGE

It's not a question of whether to change, but whether we can control the way we are changing. We are living in an *Alice in Wonderland* world where you have to run just to stay in place. To get anywhere, you have to run at full speed. Besides, the rules keep changing; when we stop and try to remember and enforce the old rules, we get swept back into the past, lose contact with the here and now. Since we do not perceive the new realities, we cannot change our behavior to cope with the demands of the external world.

In order to meet the new demands, we must first identify alternative courses of action. The more different alternatives we can find, the more likely it is that one, or a combination of several, will work for us. Second, we must identify resources. The richer the reservoir of available resources, the more likely that satisfactory solutions can be found. Third, we have to make decisions. This implies a conscious effort to make a choice rather than to allow the flow of time and events to make the decision for us. Finally, we can find ways to act on the decision. As those who have given up smoking several times know, failure to change is often the result of an inability to act on decisions rather than an inability to decide.

GENERATING ALTERNATIVES

How do you send love to someone far away? Do you send a card? Write a letter? Telephone? Telegraph flowers? By brainstorming, our own classroom groups have been able to come up with as many as sixty different ways to send love to someone far away, and they have done it in only four or five minutes. Of course, some of the ways are probably not practicable, such as sky writing, a television commercial, or ESP. But others may be useful at least some of the time: send your children, agree to watch the same TV show at the same time and think of each other, place an ad in the local newspaper of the loved ones far away, place their name on a free sample or junk mail list, or have a billboard erected telling of your love. Still, mostly we send cards; sometimes we call; occasionally we send flowers. In 1974, over 2½ billion Christmas cards were sent through the public mails in the United States. There's nothing wrong with Christmas cards, but this is an indication that we tend to think and act within a much narrower range of alternatives than need be.

Probably the most effective method for generating alternatives is brainstorming. It is designed to produce a large body of data which can later be worked on and refined. For a full discussion of brainstorming and the rules of brainstorming, see pages 38-43.

IDENTIFYING RESOURCES

The key to discovering new resources is in looking at the world from a new angle. For instance, we are just beginning to tap the great reserve of teaching potential that comes through peer instruction and cross-age helping. These are great resources that were structured out of existence by such efficiency methods of education as grade levels, homogeneous groupings, and division of college-preparatory and vocational schools.

Another great resource is the community. Seen formerly as a place for field trips — regarded as frills — the community setting is now beginning to offer to some students a reason to stay in school, a rationale for learning to read and add, etc. Furthermore, the community is full of individuals — parents, older brothers and sisters, friends, professional and business people — who possess special skills and knowledge which they are eager to share with others.

For example, suppose that Sally, a high school sophomore, checks out of school in the middle of the morning to show her younger brother's fifth grade class her slides of Canada, or her special way of knitting scarves. Imagine the self-esteem that Sally gains, the respect that her brother gains for her, and the new insights that the fifth graders gain from this resource. It is not unusual that Jenny's mother comes in to help the third grade children make cookies; why can't Bill's father come in to talk to the eleventh grade about financing a car?

What are the other resources close at hand? Look at the school office, the cafeteria, the kitchen, the furnace room.

Why can't the students poll the kitchen staff, asking for their ranking of three important issues in a forthcoming election, or find out how much fuel the building consumes per day and determine the per pupil cost of heating the building, or do a time and motion study of the school principal?

Another potential source of educational materials is the wastebasket. What do we regularly throw away that could be useful? Popsicle sticks? Styrofoam cups? Computer print-out paper? Egg cartons? The list goes on and on. Start with the material and force-fit an educational use. *How can I use popsicle sticks in English class?* Write a vocabulary word on each stick, put them in a big tin can, shake them about, and ask each student to draw one. *How can I use old computer print-outs in history class?* Have the students make a time line of events in the Civil War and another of events in the Vietnam War, then display the two charts one above the other.

Many of these proposals represent a kind of backward planning. That is, we start with a resource, try to look at it from a new angle and see what crazy schemes we can devise for it, and only then decide whether the schemes fit some of our educational goals. This method represents a deliberate deferring of evaluation while we are identifying new resources. All too often, when we establish an objective, our thinking becomes ultrarational, and we limit ourselves to the boundaries of the known. Backwards planning opens up a whole new range of creative resources.

However, there's no point in having the students count the cars on the street or make masks out of egg cartons just because these resources are available. Only when these activities can be seen as learning opportunities which match the objectives of the class can they be included as a legitimate part of the school day.

DECISION MAKING

No matter how objective the criteria seem to be, decisions are always based on value judgments. Take admissions to college, for example: If the admissions officials decide to use strictly objective measurements such as College Entrance Examination Board test scores and grade-point averages from applicants' high schools, then they are placing a positive value on these measurements as opposed to other criteria they could use (principal's recommendation, interview, autobiographical letter, color of eyes, length of hair, etc.). The admissions officers may choose "objective" criteria because (1) they believe that these will result in the type of person they desire as students, or (2) these are the only feasible criteria to process under the pressures of time and resources, or (3) these are the criteria that have "always been used." Whatever the reasons are for selecting a particular set of criteria, the fact remains that the decision is based on value judgments, either conscious or unconscious.

The same is true when we buy a car. Our decision may be based on objective criteria such as price, mechanical performance, and style, but when we select these as criteria we are placing a value on money, dependability, speed, cornering, and so forth. There is no decision which is not founded on value judgment.

If all decisions are based on value-related criteria, two implications follow: First, effective decision making is more likely to take place when the values underlying the available options are explored and clarified. Second, an individual will be best served by his decision when the criteria are based on an awareness and understanding of the end goals of that decision.

In the case of the admissions officers, if the end goal of the admissions procedure is to select students who are capable of doing the academic work of the college, the appropriate criteria are those which best determine who is academically capable. If, on the other hand, the end goal of the admissions officers is to find those persons who can best use the college experience to promote their own social-self-actualization for the benefit of society, another set of criteria may be more appropriate than the College Board scores.

Similarly, if our end goal for a new car is to provide reliable, comfortable transportation, then our criteria for decision making may be quite different than if our end goal is to get transportation as cheaply as possible, or if our end goal is to enhance our self-images and our feelings of prestige and worthiness in the eyes of our peers.

There is a third important element in effective decision making: the identification of creative alternatives. Whenever a problem is close and persistent, it is easy to get locked into a narrow range of options. For instance, when we were shopping for an automobile recently, we felt that one of the essential requirements was more space for our growing family. We also wanted something that was small for city driving and economical on gas. At some point in our deliberations, we seemed to get locked into thinking only of new compact imported station wagons. We looked at many varieties but didn't seem to find the one that was right for us. Tired and frustrated, we decided to put off the job of getting a new car for a month or two. During that hiatus we had a chance to explore some of our values. Did it have to be new? Imported? A station wagon? And what were all the things we wanted the car to do? When we went back to shopping seriously, we quickly homed in on the right car for us: a new, imported, medium-sized, two-door sedan with a very large trunk. We had gotten away from the problem enough to break our narrow, locked-in pattern of thinking, and we had given ourselves a chance to clarify just what our end goals of buying a car really were.

Formal decision making can be seen as a four-step process: First, identify the end goals of the decision and rank them in order of importance to the decision maker. Second, list all available options, including wild, unrealistic ideas wherever possible because, as in brainstorming sessions, these far-out ideas often contain the germ of some new creative and workable option. Third, examine the values, the benefits and weaknesses, of each of the options. Finally, match the values of each option with the end goals. Which options seem likely to lead most directly to the end goals? Is there a creative blend of options which can serve the end goals better than the individual options as listed?

Of course, most decisions are not made as a result of such formal deliberations. The important things are an awareness of our end goals and a realization of our power of seeking creative options to meet them.

ACTIVITIES FOR DECISION MAKING

Subject: *Decision Charting.*

Material: Blackboard, chalk, paper, pencils.

Procedure:

1. Divide the blackboard into four columns. The first column is labeled *Ranking,* the second *End Goals,* the third *Options,* and the fourth *Option Values.*

2. With the class, select a decision area for study: to buy a car, to choose what to do after high school, to choose a course of study, etc.

3. The students brainstorm possible end goals of that decision area, with the teacher recording items on the board in the second column.

4. Students are asked to rank the end goals in order of importance to them, first individually on paper, and then as a group. Record these in column 1.

5. The class brainstorms a list of options that might be available for the decision.

6. Those options that seem most useful are then selected for further work, and are listed in column 3. The values inherent in each of these options are listed in column 4.

7. Now the decision makers have before them a great quantity of information organized in a meaningful fashion. By comparing the option values with the important end goals, they can determine which of the available options is likely to prove most appropriate (see diagram below).

Decision Charting			
DECISION: Buying a Car			
Ranking	*End Goals*	*Options*	*Option Values*
1	transportation	economy car	money, parking
2	fun	sports car	impress others, have fun
4	feeling of importance		
5	to impress others	fix up junked car	fun to do
3	make money with	station wagon	use to carry stuff
	etc.	etc.	etc.

Subject: *Force-Field Analysis.*

Material: Blackboard, chalk.

NOTE: When an either-or decision is to be faced, such as going to college or getting a job, quitting smoking or continuing smoking, buying a record or putting the money in a savings account, then the problem can be looked at as a field of opposing forces, some pulling in one direction, some in the other.

Procedure:

1. Divide the blackboard into two columns, each labeled with one of the two choices.

2. The class brainstorms all the forces pulling in one direction, the teacher recording each item.

3. The class brainstorms all the forces pulling in the other direction, and the teacher records these in the other column.

4. Now the students can rank the two lists of forces in order of strength (or importance). Once again, much of the information which affects the decision has been organized and displayed in a useful way (see diagram on page 216).

NOTE: These activities also have a wide range of usefulness in less personal contexts, particularly in the social studies. In many cases, the situation becomes a modified role play. Decision Charting is a useful tool, for instance, in dealing with a local or federal agency's handling of a pollution problem, or of a mayor's approach to urban transportation. Force-field analysis can be applied to the specifics of either of those problems, and it can be widely used in analyzing the decisions of historical and literary figures, such as Napoleon's decision to march to Moscow or Sidney Carton's decision at the end of *A Tale of Two Cities.*

Force-Field Analysis	
DECISION: *Smoking*	
FORCES COMPELLING ME TO CONTINUE	FORCES COMPELLING ME TO GIVE IT UP
taste	health
use in social situations	parents
makes me feel grown up	cost
keeps mosquitoes away in summer	can't taste food as well
keeps my weight down	smells up my clothes
etc.	etc.

Subject: *Decisions Role Plays.*

Material: Two chairs.

Procedure:

1. Two chairs are set out, one representing *Cautious Bill*, the other *Adventurous Bill.* The two halves of Bill carry on a dialogue about whether he should spend the summer at home cutting grass and earning money or hitchhike across the country.

2. The members of the class are divided in half, one group supplying the dialogue for Cautious Bill, the other half for Adventurous Bill.

3. This role play provides a great deal of useful data, and is most effective when followed by a discussion which focuses on both the specific decisions involved and the decision-making process.

NOTE: In a short role play, two persons can try to convince each other of the value of going to college, on the one hand, or getting a job, on the other. Or one person can play both roles, moving back and forth between two chairs, one marked *to quit smoking* and the other *to continue smoking.*

ACTING ON DECISIONS

It's relatively easy to decide—what's hard is to act on those decisions. Old habits are hard to break. Established relationships work toward self-preservation. Any change in a pattern of behavior is likely to lead to such a general uneasiness that the change cannot be tolerated.

For instance, nothing much has been changed in the secondary school curriculum: We still think in terms of pre-established categories — English, math, history. Instead of revising our thinking about curricular development, we have tried to add things — sex education, drug education, driver education, group counseling. We tuck all these new and important additions to the curriculum into the cracks and corners of an already overstuffed day.

We've made enough decisions about what we *do* need to teach. What we must do is make some hard decisions about what *not* to teach, what to pull out of the curriculum so that the school experience is once again comprehensible. The same is true of our personal lives. A writer may feel himself getting flabby as he sits at his typewriter exercising only his fingers. But by the time he's finished his working day, he's too tired for exercises. If he's serious about adopting a daily routine, then he must decide what it is that he can eliminate from his daily schedule — or else find a way to do two things at once.

The second part of acting on decisions is sticking with the new decision long enough for it to become established as a new pattern of behavior. Maxwell Maltz in *Psycho-Cybernetics*[1] suggests that about three weeks are required for a new pattern of behavior to become established. So if you are quitting smoking, try to last for a three-week period, counting the days. It may get easier after that. For more complex changes, the period of adjustment may be longer. The New York City School System is said to have tried every educational reform in existence — for one week. When the reform didn't produce results in the short run, it was rejected. Eliminate grades, and you may have parents and students on your back for a whole year, maybe two. Significant change, radical change, needs time to become established.

Notes

1.   Englewood Cliffs, N. J., Prentice-Hall, 1960.

Part III
Notes on Teaching for Personal and Social Growth

Chapter Ten

POSITIVE FOCUS

If you ask a teenager to list his personal strengths on one side of a page and then turn the paper over and list his weaknesses, chances are that he will come up with about six items on the strengths side, but that he'll write about 40 on the weakness side.[1] Our culture focuses so heavily on the negative, on weaknesses, on what we can't do, that there is little time left to build on the positive, on our strengths, on what we *can* do. And the average classroom is no exception, reflecting the focus of the larger culture not only in the attitude of the students and of the teacher toward themselves, but in the way that students relate to one another, to the teacher, and to the school.

In an experiment designed to show the effect of positive and negative personal feedback,[2] a class at a major Eastern university, a graduate history section of about 20 students, was given special instructions. The professor, unaware that he was being videotaped by a concealed camera, began his lecture head down, hands grasping the lectern, reading from his notes in a monotone. The students sprawled in various postures of inattention and boredom. At a pre-arranged moment, the students started to act more interested in the lecture — they sat up, nodded their heads, smiled, leaned forward, and gave other non-verbal signs of interest and support. Like a flower unfolding, the professor moved away from the podium, began to use his hands in expressive gestures, spoke more energetically, and developed eye contact with members of the class. At a clandestine signal, however, the students returned to their original postures of boredom and inattention. In less than three minutes, the professor was back behind the safety of his desk, hands clenching the lectern, droning on from his lecture notes, a withered shadow of the person he had been.

This is what we can do for each other: we can enhance each other's lives, build on each other's strengths, or we can tear each other down, enervate and cripple.

EVALUATING STUDENT ACHIEVEMENT

Teachers are seemingly forced into providing negative focus. Grading compositions, correcting tests, checking spelling, diagnosing reading problems — all have a distinctly negative focus, and all are at least as damaging as they may be beneficial. Not only do these practices diminish the students' feelings of self-esteem, but when a teacher identifies a learning deficiency such as a "spelling problem" or a "reading problem," this labeling in effect lets the "problem" become the teacher's; responsibility for learning subtly shifts from the student to the teacher. (This may be one reason that remedial reading programs have in general been so abysmally ineffective: when a student is classed as a "remedial reader," he realizes that he has a special problem about which he really can do nothing without the help of an expert. The problem of dyslexia will not be resolved until it is seen as one aspect of a larger problem which also includes a lack of self-respect, feelings of powerlessness, etc.)

Grades foster a negative focus. Even an A-minus is a sign of negativity. Points are always taken *off.* Standardized testing is another school institution that often focuses on the negative: Did you realize that 49 percent-plus of the school population is below average on any given standardized achievement test? A third generally negative focus in the school situation is the use of comments instead of or in addition to grades. Teachers almost always feel that they must make a balanced comment, stressing both the strengths and the weaknesses of the student.

A GROWTH-ENHANCING ENVIRONMENT

How can we build a classroom climate that is positive and growth-enhancing? How can we and our students learn to identify and build on our own strengths and the strengths of others? We see two stages — first, to foster an awareness of the prevailing negative focus to the degree that it exists; second, to develop skills in positive focus.

One useful technique for developing awareness is brainstorming. The class can be asked to brainstorm for five minutes all the things that students can do to each other and that teachers can do to students that get students down on themselves or create feelings of defensiveness. Then, another five minutes can be spent brainstorming all the things that students can do that raise feelings of self-esteem and supportiveness. A general discussion can follow, focusing on what changes will make the students and teacher more supportive of each other.

Another possibility is to ask the students to brainstorm all the self-put-downs that they can think of — that is, all the things they can say and think about themselves that make them feel less worthy. Next, they should brainstorm all the things students can think about themselves that make them feel more powerful, more worthy. This can be followed by a discussion of why we put ourselves down so much and how we can change.

For the second stage, developing skills in positive focus, perhaps the first thing is to stress that positive focus can be considered a skill and, just as in learning a new game, no one is expected to be perfect at first. A second step is to ask the students to monitor their own self-put-downs and to try to change to statements of self-affirmation. Students can try to catch each other at self-put-downs: "I'm hearing you putting yourself down. That's against the rules in this class." And as a forfeit, when a student is caught putting himself down, he must frame a statement of self-affirmation. The other students can help: "I caught you putting yourself down; now you have to make a self-affirming statement. 'I like the way I smile.' 'I like the way I listen.' 'I like the way I stand up for what I think is right.' How about one of those?"

A third way to practice skills in positive focus is for the teacher to call for a validating round, an exercise which promotes verbal expression of appreciation for others. Validating rounds generally come at the end of small group discussions of personal topics such as "My happiest moment from early childhood," or "The one day I would like to live over again because it was just about perfect," or "If I could do anything I wanted to for two whole days, I'd . . ." Or, the validating round can occur after the students have read their compositions to each other in small groups or tried to reach consensus on a forced-choice problem. For the procedure, see the Activity section of this chapter, page 234.

Positive focus requires practice and faith. It is not easy to go counter to the general norms of our culture and the beliefs and attitudes of so many of our fellow humans. But over time, a continuing and steadfast focus on the positive in life, on our strengths, and on the strengths of others, can help to restore in our students their energy, their feelings of power, their sense of worth, so that they can contribute to the task of building a better world.

ACTIVITIES FOR DEVELOPING POSITIVE FOCUS SKILLS

Subject: *People and Places Questionnaire.*

Material: *People and Places Questionnaires* (one copy for each student — see page 229), pencils or pens, stack of blank postcards (optional).

Procedure:

1. The teacher might wish to present a short talk on

positive focus, stressing skill building and the dangers of trying to maintain a "balanced" outlook in a world where "balancing" will inevitably throw the focus strongly on the negative.

2. The teacher divides the class into small groups of three or four.

3. The *Questionnaires* are distributed and the teacher asks that the students work by themselves for four minutes, trying to answer as many of the questions as possible.

4. After the four minutes, the teacher asks the students to review their lists, placing a mark beside any question they did not answer or beside any answer that seems unsatisfactory to them.

5. The teacher asks the students to spend the next five minutes working in small groups helping each member to identify new answers or to improve on those answers with which he is dissatisfied.

6. Each student marks the three questions that have produced the most vivid, pleasant memories.

7. After the students have spent one or two minutes reviewing and marking their questions, the teacher asks the group members to share with each other one or two of those pleasant memories that have been evoked by this activity. Students should budget their own time so that each person in the group will have a chance to speak during the allotted time (usually about ten minutes).

8. As an optional addition, the teacher might place a stack of postcards on a table and invite the students to practice their skill of giving positive reinforcement to others by writing a postcard to one of the persons whose name appears on the questionnaire. The teacher may point out that an easy way to begin such a postcard is "We were doing this activity in class, and my teacher gave us postcards to write to people, so here is one."

People and Places Questionnaire

Directions: This is a private questionnaire for your own use. No one will collect it at the end of the period or ask to see it. Read over the questions below and jot down answers to any you can. Later you and the others in your group may help each other and discuss this activity, but right now work alone.

1. Who gives you a lift—someone who makes you feel good just to see him or her coming?

2. Who is a good listener—someone who really pays attention and really hears what you have to say?

3. Who is the best teacher you ever had—someone whom you'd like to learn from again and again?

4. Who has been a big help to you—someone who really came through or stood by you when you needed it?

5. What older person do you admire—someone of your parents' generation that you'd really want to be like?

6. What person in an occupational capacity has done a good deed for you recently—a storekeeper, policeman, teacher, bus driver, or someone else who has helped you out while doing his job?

7. Who, if the telephone was to ring right now, would you like to talk to?

8. Where have you been that you would like to go back to and spend a week doing just as you wished?

9. Where was it that you last laughed until it hurt?

10. What place away from home makes you feel when you go there that you really belong?

11. Where away from home did you have the nicest meal recently?

12. What place outdoors would you like to go and spend a whole day?

Subject: *Support Brainstorm and Letter Writing.*

Material: Postcards, envelopes, letter paper, stamps, address lists (see NOTE below), pencils or pens.

Procedure:

1. The class is divided into groups of four to six students.

2. Each group brainstorms for five minutes the names of public figures whom they support for some recent action.

3. The recorder from each group then reads the list to the entire class, the members of the class having been asked to listen carefully to all the lists so that they can select individually one, two, or three persons from all the lists whom they really support for some action.

4. After the lists have been read to the entire class, each group member is asked to tell his group the one, two, or three (but never more than three) persons whom he chooses to support.

5. Then each group decides what to do with that information, the teacher giving the following options:

    a. Reach consensus as a group on one public figure to whom the group will compose and send a letter of support.

    b. Reach consensus as a group and then send a letter listing your reasons for support to the local newspaper.

    c. Subdivide your group into smaller groups, each of which composes and sends a letter either to the person or to the newspaper.

    d. Work individually on letters as above.

e.   Some other course of supportive action.

f.   Nothing at all.

NOTE: The teacher should supply himself with as many sources of addresses as possible, or be able to provide the students with the location of address sources. Addresses of political figures, sports figures, movie and TV figures are especially useful, and generally mail will be forwarded to these persons from official offices, team headquarters, studios, etc.

Subject: *Personal Attributes.*

Material: *Personal Attribute Worksheets* (see page 233), one copy per student; pencils or pens.

Procedure:

1.   The teacher hands out the *Personal Attributes Worksheets* and asks each student to rank order the ten attributes in order of importance to the individual.

2.   Groups of four to six are formed, and each student is encouraged to share with the others an experience where one of his three top-ranked attributes played an important role.

3.   If there is time at the end of the sharing, the group may try to reach consensus on a ranking of the attributes in order of importance to the group. Then the group may wish to discuss what the ranking might be for the society at large (or for segments of it, such as parents of group members, teachers, policemen, public figures, etc.).

Personal Attribute Worksheet

Directions: Rank order these ten attributes in order of their importance to you:

YOUR RANKING	ATTRIBUTE
	a. Adventurous
	b. Ambitious
	c. Competitive
	d. Considerate
	e. Creative
	f. Helpful
	g. Independent
	h. Intelligent
	i. Responsible
	j. Self-controlled

Now write the three highest ranked attributes in the spaces below. For each attribute, think of one incident from your life where it played an important role.

1. _____

2. _____

3. _____

Share as many of these incidents as you wish with the others in your group.

Subject: *Validating Rounds.*[3]

Material: Paper, pencils.

Procedure:

1.   The class is divided into small groups, preferably of four or five.

2.   To begin the validating round, each person writes the name of each of the other persons in the group, skipping four lines between names.

3.   The teacher asks the students to write two positive statements about each of the other students in the group, being as specific as possible. They may use, if they wish, some of the following sentence starters: *I like the way you . . .* or *You're a lot like me when you . . .* or *It made me feel good when you said . . .* or *You are. . . .*

4.   The teacher should remind the students that this is a skill-building exercise: they are probably going to feel uncomfortable reading each of their validating statements, and it most likely will seem embarrassing to a student to hear his classmates read to him.

5.   Then the teacher asks that in each group the students focus on one person at a time and everybody read his validating statements about that person. Then the focus moves to the next person, and so on around the group.

Many people are unable to believe or even to *hear* good things said about themselves. The teacher should ask students to try to avoid the "Aw, shucks, it's really nothing" or the "Oh, I'm not really all that" behavior when it is their turn to be the focus person. One final rule: You must *mean* what you say.

CAUTION: "Validating Rounds" is an important and powerful activity. It should be used only when the class understands fully the concepts of positive focus and the importance of an accepting, positive regard for each individual. This rarely occurs in the first session.

Also, it is important to allow enough time to complete this activity within the class period. Generally, twenty minutes is enough for a group of four, especially if the teacher warns the class of the time five minutes before the bell. If there is not enough time for the validating round, it is better to postpone it until the start of the next day's class.

Notes

1.   Unpublished study conducted by Dr. Herbert Otto.

2.   Described to us by David D. Britton, to whom we are indebted for introducing us to the notion of positive focus and to much of the material in this chapter.

3.   This activity owes its inspiration to Sidney B. Simon's elaboration on the validating principles in Harvey Jackins' re-evaluation counseling technique.

Chapter Eleven

GRADES AND EVALUATION

Fantasy: It's payday, and the workers are standing around the cashier's office talking in small groups. Smith goes up to the window, gets his pay envelope, rips it open eagerly and exclaims: "Two hundred dollars! Wow, I really hit it this week! Boy, did I fool that old bat. Hey, Brown, how much did you get?" Brown looks at him sullenly, "Twenty-eight dollars. That bastard had it in for me this week. I couldn't do anything right for her." Smith grins: "It's not what you do, it's how you do it. Give her a little of the old brown nose like I do."

Suppose just for an instant that people in real life were graded just like kids in school and paid accordingly. The boss keeps her idea of how much you should get in a little black book full of letters and numbers. She averages the number of fenders that you were able to put on during the test period with your score on the welding proficiency test (WPT), adds in the scores that she pulled out of the air for the three times she called on you to check your work, and throws in an attitude grade and perhaps something for effort. Then she adds it all up, averages it, and converts it to dollars of pay. If you don't think it was fair, you can always complain to the supervisor, but it's his job to back her up, and he always does.

We expect that if people in the real world were graded like kids in school, we would see an alarming jump in the number of assaults, murders, suicides, and divorces per year. Grades just aren't very fair, and the wonder of it is that students put up with them as peaceably as they do.

The litany against grading is long and passionate.[1] The following is a brief synopsis of the major arguments for abolishing the grading system.

1. *Grades are quixotic—not tied to reality.* *Some* test scores are reliable measures for measuring *some* specific things. But the practice of using a variety of unreliable measures (grades on homework, tests, compositions, class participation, effort), then weighting those measures according to the teacher's hunch (tests count two-thirds, homework one-sixth, effort and class participation one-sixth, etc.), and finally giving a comprehensive score for "English" or "Math" or whatever, produces a score that is of doubtful validity as a measure of anything.

2. *Grades shift the locus of evaluation from the person himself to an external agency.* This erodes our creativity and our self-motivation. Of course, others, including the teacher, provide a valuable source of feedback as the individual shapes his life. But creative, self-motivated, self-directed people are not produced by procedures which

corrupt that internal feeling that this is good and right for me not because someone else says so, but because my guts and my brain tell me so.

3. *Grades extinguish internal motivation.* There is clear evidence that external rewards and punishments shift the locus of motivation from the intrinsic reward of doing a worthwhile task well to the external motivation of gaining a reward or avoiding a penalty. In a controlled study, one group of students was given a set of puzzle blocks which most people would consider intrinsically interesting and paid a sum of money for each correct solution. The other group was given the same blocks and asked to do the same puzzles. In the "rest period" after each group had done its work, the group which had not been paid continued to work on the puzzle, finding new and intriguing solutions. The other group showed little interest in the blocks once they had been paid. Clearly the intrinsic motivation, the natural curiosity and delight in discovery, had been extinguished in the paid group.

When we pay our students with grades, we do much the same thing. It is worthwhile to note, however, that praise does not have the same effect as money. In the same block experiment, another group of students who were given verbal rewards showed the same continuing interest in the blocks as the group which got no reward or money. The notion, expressed by many people, that praise has the same effect as tangible reward is apparently incorrect. Verbal praise acts as feedback which increases self-esteem and reinforces internal motivation.

4. *Grades shift the responsibility for learning from the*

student to the teacher. With the emphasis on grades, the student is motivated toward getting a good grade rather than toward learning something. It becomes the teacher's responsibility to structure the curriculum so that what the student does to get a good grade is also what the student should be doing in order to learn. This places a double burden on the teacher, and the student is left with the job of figuring out what he should be doing in order to get a good grade.

5. *Grades shift the role of the teacher from helper to judge.* How much will you trust your lawyer if you know that he is also your only jury? To what extent does this limit your ability to confide in him? To what extent does it motivate you toward buttering him up rather than being honest with him?

6. *Grades debase potentially meaningful work.* For example, one way to let students engage in meaningful writing for potentially responsive audiences is to encourage letter writing. But if the letter must be checked over by the teacher for spelling, mechanics, and style, the letter becomes an exercise for English class instead of being a real letter to a real Bobby Orr, Raquel Welch, or Senator Church.

A sort of inverse proof of this point is that the things we don't grade become unimportant in the students' eyes. We don't grade original poetry ("How can you grade a poem?") and so the writing of poetry becomes unimportant ("I scribbled something down and then spent extra time on my math because we were getting a grade on that.").

7. *Grading narrows the focus of teaching concerns to*

those things which can be easily graded. This is probably the reason that so much grammar is taught and math is taught as a series of problems requiring solutions. Grading leads teachers to teach those things which can be graded (multiplication facts, comma rules, causes of the Civil War, second conjugation verbs, etc.) rather than those that defy grades (ethics, logic, ability to empathize, collaboration, self-motivation, etc.). It is characteristic of many schools today to have a statement of purpose which reflects the ideals of teaching for personal and social growth, but to have a curriculum in which that kind of teaching is unlikely to occur.

8. *Finally, grades foster a competitive, win-lose atmosphere.* When students wave their hands eagerly to answer the teacher's question, it is often not because they want to share an insight with the class but because they want to have the teacher recognize their superiority. They want to say it first. For those who argue that competition is basically healthy, we answer that competition is so pervasive, so ingrained in our society, that there is no need to fear that it will die. For instance, television, with its advertising, talk shows, and football games, is a huge teaching machine, teaching competitive values that no amount of formal schooling is going to eradicate. The value of de-emphasizing competition in school is to redress the balance somewhat.

In addition, the whole system of grades supports an erroneous conception of growth and the learning processes. Natural growth does not take place on a constant upward incline, but rather by fits and starts, with regressions and plateaus. Indiscriminate grading that catches one student during a spurt and another at a regression point leaves the impression that one is smarter than the other, has learned more, or has worked harder. The student who is tested at a regression point may be so demoralized that his entire academic career and perhaps his whole life is affected. A low grade leads to a low self-evaluation of the individual's own abilities which leads to low effort on his part, which leads to low achievement which leads to another low grade . . .

GRADING VS. EVALUATION

The fact that administrators, teachers, parents, and students have come to accept grades, to rely on grades, to want grades, and in fact to feel that they *need* grades does not make it any more permissible to continue this invidious practice. It is almost a case of the prisoners who have come to rely on their chains and thus fear freedom. Grades have no socially redeeming value. Grades are not a useful motivator, they are not a useful evaluator, they are not a useful predictor, they are not a useful separator. Grades must be abolished.

Evaluation, on the other hand, must *not* be abolished. Evaluation is an important and useful activity in living and learning. Evaluation is the process of placing values on past events by means of analysis and diagnosis, and of placing values on future events by setting goals. Because it is based on value judgments, evaluation is a basically human rather than mechanical activity. So the fundamental questions for evaluators are first, "What are our goals?" and then, "Are we achieving these goals?"

Generally, in education evaluation we use inappropriate

and inaccurate instruments to diagnose and measure our achievements. Furthermore, most of our reliable evaluative instruments are designed to measure short-term learning while completely ignoring the long-term effects of a given practice. For instance, we measure young people for their skill and understanding in reading. But we seldom evaluate whether our teaching methods will lead our students to enjoy reading and to consider it a useful part of their lives. How many people dread having to write a letter because of the way they were taught composition, or hate the thought of balancing their checkbook because of their early experience in learning addition?

ACTIVITY FOR EVALUATION

Subject: *Evaluation Brainstorming*

Material: Paper and pencils or pens.

Procedure:

1. The teacher instructs the students to brainstorm for five minutes the ways in which they want people to be different after any chosen learning experience.

2. Next, students are instructed to select no more than three items on their list as most important.

3. The class is asked to brainstorm for five minutes

behaviors that they would be willing to accept as evidence that the experience was successful — that is, that people are really different in the ways determined in Procedure Step No. 2.

4. The class brainstorms, again for five minutes, behaviors that could be regarded as evidence that the experience was not successful — that is, that people have not changed as determined in No. 2.

5. The class brainstorms (five minutes) ways of collecting the evidence listed in Steps 3 and 4.

6. The class brainstorms (five minutes) ways of displaying evidence so that it is meaningful to someone else.

7. The class is instructed to go back over the material in the previous items and design an evaluation program which they and/or the teacher could carry out.

NOTE: This program can be used for very narrow goals (*I want people to be different by being able to recite the nines table, which they could not do before*), or the program can be used for larger goals (*I want people to be different by being able to make more rational decisions about their lives than they could do before*). Step 5 can include the use of standardized tests (*I will collect evidence that the students have learned multiplication by their performance on the Stanford Achievement test*), or it can use subjective or unobtrusive measure (*I will collect evidence that students have improved their use of empathetic understanding by*

*counting the frequency of put-down statements per hour of
class time*).

NOTE: This procedure can also be used effectively by a
committee of teachers or by an individual teacher working
alone.

GRADES AND EVALUATION ALTERNATIVES

Resourceful teachers have come up with creative alternatives
which can work within the grading system and yet soften its
damaging effects. Here are three resourceful alternatives
which make use of more traditional grading schemes, the first
of which is included in a letter to the authors from Reed
Hankwitz, a teacher of math and foreign languages at Friends
Academy, North Dartmouth, Massachusetts.

"Our school finally reduced marks to A, B, C, D, F —
simply those letters, with no +'s or -'s. (We also mark effort
and citizenship, but that's beside the point.) This simplifica-
tion enabled me to dream up my own scheme for grading
with increased understanding (I hope) for all concerned. Here
it is:

"Those who don't work get F.
"Those who work and—
     spend most of their time (more than half) master-
     ing (?) the fundamentals (as shown on quizzes) get:
         D if they fail more quizzes than they pass.
         C if they pass more quizzes than they fail.

spend most of their time (after mastering funda-
mentals) on applications thereof, get:

> B if their applications are par for the course.
> A if their applications are mostly based on
> "advanced work," i.e. concepts or techniques
> considered beyond the usual scope of the
> present course.

"I have chosen to apply this system on a weekly basis, as
far as the judging of time (more or less than half, etc.) is
concerned, and then simply to average 'weeks' for a term
grade. Since my quizzes are 'pass/fail,' there's almost no
nit-picking about marks, and each student can readily see at
any time just where he stands from the work he's doing."

David Bergman of North Quincy High School (Massachusetts) uses a complex *Student Grade Analysis* which is
reproduced on page 247. In this system each of several
criteria, such as attendance, work completion, quality of
work, class participation, effort, and level of study, is given a
separate point scale, and the individual student is rated along
each of these scales. One advantage of such a system is that
the grading values of the teacher or school stand out clearly.
For instance, attendance is clearly the most important value
in Mr. Bergman's scheme because it is given a maximum of
forty points while the next highest value, work completion, is
given a maximum of twenty points. Using this format, any
individual teacher, department, or school can devise a grade
analysis system which will reflect its own values.

An elaboration of David Bergman's system could be to
have the class as a whole reach consensus on the value of each
of the criteria, and the rating scale could be revised to reflect

those values. Individuals could design their own rating scales (with the advice and consent of the teacher, perhaps, so that realistic limits are set on the value of any one criterion—e.g. valuing perfect attendance as 95 might seem unrealistic to some). The class might brainstorm other criteria to be used in place of or in addition to some of those on Mr. Bergman's analysis sheet.

Dietrich August reports that at the Eaglebrook School in Deerfield, Mass., each department determines its own grading scheme. Thus a student's report card might carry letter grades in one subject, percentage grades in another, and pass/fail in a third. Mr. August reports that the Eaglebrook English department has adopted the pass/fail system with the criterion for failure that a student makes so little effort that his instructor can be of no help to him.

One more solution to the problem of coping with the grading system is to use the *Individual Study Contract* (see page 249). At the beginning of each unit of study, or at the beginning of an independent study project, each student fills out an *Individualized Study Contract*. These can be prepared by individuals with or without the advice of the teacher, or time can be set aside for groups of three or four to work on study contracts with one person being the focus while others in the group give him advice. The process is repeated until everyone in the group has been the focus for help.

Individualized Study Contracts should be open to renegotiation at any time during the study period. Students may have a real need to change or abandon a project as they learn more about that project. The value of sticking to something until it is finished can lead to costly mistakes.

Student Grade Analysis

_____ _____
NAME   TITLE OF COURSE

_____ _____
INSTRUCTOR   MARKING PERIOD ENDING

Attendance

Excellent 40

Good 30

Fair 20

Poor 10

Fail 0

Attendance points _____

Quality of Work

Excellent 10

Always good 8

Sometimes good 5

Fair 4

Poor 0

Quality points _____

Work Completion

All 20

Most 15

Some 10

Little 5

None 0

Completion points _____

Class Participation

Makes significant
contribution 10

Questions where
applicable 8

Answers when
questioned 7

Attentive 5

Not attentive 0

Participation points _____

Effort	Level of Study
Works to best of ability 10	Difficult—college 10
Works when motivated 8	Requires research 8
Makes some effort 5	Average difficulty 5
Makes little effort 3	Material is basic 3
Makes no effort 0	Insignificant 0
Effort points ____	Level points ____

Extra credit _____   _____
criteria   points

TOTAL GRADE _____

Another valuable tool in evaluation is feedback in various forms. All of the types of feedback described in Chapter Five (see pages 83-101) can provide valuable insights to both teachers and students.

Individualized Study Contract

_____   _____ / _____
NAME   STUDENT'S SIGNATURE   DATE

_____   _____ / _____
SPONSORING INSTRUCTOR   INSTRUCTOR'S SIGNATURE   DATE

_____
BRIEF DESCRIPTIVE TITLE

Statement of objectives: Use additional paper if necessary.

Activities planned:

Names of collaborators (if any):

Evaluation criteria: (Paper, oral report, portfolio, journal of activities, discussion with instructor, tape recording, film, etc.)

Criteria for grading: Be as specific as possible.

Projected completion date: *Grade:*

Teacher Self-Evaluation Form

1. Community – atmosphere of acceptance, trust, openness.

1	2	3	4	5	6	7

LOW   HIGH

2. Achievement motivation – (a) students involved in setting goals.

1	2	3	4	5	6	7

LOW   HIGH

3. Achievement motivation – (b & c) students involved in setting procedures and conditions.

1	2	3	4	5	6	7

LOW   HIGH

4. Awareness of student concerns.

1	2	3	4	5	6	7

LOW   HIGH

5. Self-renewal – utilization of variety of learning styles and settings.

1	2	3	4	5	6	7

LOW   HIGH

6. Presence of creativity.

| 1 | 2 | 3 | 4 | 5 | 6 | 7 |

LOW   HIGH

7. Atmosphere of joy and vitality.

| 1 | 2 | 3 | 4 | 5 | 6 | 7 |

LOW   HIGH

In addition, the teacher can apply several types of self-evaluation such as the *Teacher Self-Evaluation Form* (see page 250) and the use of anecdotal records. The *Teacher Self-Evaluation Form* can be used daily for certain periods or weekly or by the term. The keeping of anecdotal records is an ongoing process. These are often best noted in a teacher's journal. The teacher may set aside three or four minutes after each class or at the end of the day for writing specific observations in his journal. Teachers often find that there is also time for writing in journals during class while students are engaged in small group or individual activities.

The anecdotal records should focus on description rather than simple evaluation. It is much more valuable to say, "During the small group discussion of the rank-order problem, there was much gesticulating, nodding, and smiling. Jimmy Jones took a leading role for the first time, and the class was slow to break up after the bell," rather than, "We had several lively discussions in class today."

Notes

1.   See for example, Howard Kirschenbaum, Sidney B. Simon, & Rodney W. Napier, *Wad-Ja-Get? The Grading Game in American Education* (New York, Hart, 1971). Also, William Glasser, *Schools Without Failure* (New York, Harper & Row, 1969).

Chapter Twelve

DISCIPLINE
AND
BEHAVIOR CONTROL

Discipline in the classroom is such an individual affair, so colored by the specific mix of personalities and needs, that it is almost impossible to say anything that will seem satisfactory and realistic to an individual teacher who has to cope with a specific student's behavior problem. Some rules, however, may help some individuals with specific problems.

1. *Avoid ultimatums*: "If I catch you throwing one more spitball, I'll . . ." This is almost like throwing down a gauntlet. It marks the beginning of a duel of wits in which the student can hardly lose, the teacher hardly win. The ultimatum pins down the teacher to watching especially for the given behavior, judging whether or not it really occurred ("I was just throwing it in the waste-basket so I wouldn't be tempted again"), and then facing up to fulfilling the terms of his threat, whether he wants to or not. Ultimatums almost invariably backfire, and they seldom eliminate the unwanted activity.

2. *Avoid sarcasm*: "Can't you make more noise than

that?" Students don't know how to handle sarcasm — is the teacher being nice or nasty — what does he really mean? Sarcasm makes most students feel put down and leaves them with a feeling that they need to get back somehow.

3. *When in doubt, delay.* Avoid hasty actions. There's nothing wrong with saying, "I'm really not sure just what to do about that. I'm going to think it over. In the meantime, let's go on with . . ."

4. *Try to avoid contaminating the entire life of the student.* Keep school problems at school, no matter how great the temptation is to turn the parents loose on the offender. Warnings sent home have such varied and unforeseen consequences that they are almost sure to leave a residue of resentment, which the student will sooner or later express.

5. *Look for realistic steps toward compliance.* "Sit with your hands folded in silence for the rest of the period," may seem like a good idea at the time, but "Let me have your unbroken attention for the next two minutes — Johnny, here's the stop watch, you keep time," is more likely to work.

6. *Try to understand the forces underlying acting-out behavior.* Remember that behavior is generally motivated as a means of coping with some force or forces. (Need for security? Attention? Self-respect? Love? Revenge?)

7. *Use the behavior problem as a learning experience*

wherever possible. The problem almost inevitably is the result of a conflict of wills. Try to identify what is being willed by whom, and then work for a no-lose resolution where all parties can come away with the feeling that their rights have been respected and that they have not lost self-esteem. Perhaps the most important thing that the teacher can teach is how to work on changing a conflict situation to one where each party understands and respects the other. In this way, they can work on resolving the problem rather than besting the other person.

8. *Try to avoid thinking of the student as a problem.* He may cause problems for you, but he is not *per se* a problem. If you think of a student as a problem, he is not likely to disappoint you. Teachers often unconsciously narrow the range of acceptable behaviors for problem students — they watch them more closely and find more faults as a result. It's a self-fulfilling prophecy.

9. *Take ownership of the problem.* If Billy knocks his books on the floor and disturbs the giving of instructions, the problem is yours, not his: You are the one that wants quiet so that you can be understood. (This does not imply that you are the *cause* of the unwanted behavior, only that you are the one to whom the behavior is a problem.) This changes your manner of addressing Billy from "Why can't you act your age?" or "What's the matter with you now?" to "Billy, I need you to be quiet while I'm giving directions," or "I need your help — no one will understand me if you make too much noise."

10. *Take ownership of your own feelings.*   If you are irritated and upset, say so. "I'm sorry, I feel irritated and upset because of your actions, and I'm finding it very hard to think what is the fair thing for me to do."

11. *Avoid physical and psychological force wherever possible.*   Both kinds of force drive the symptoms of basic needs underground. In an extreme case, you may have a quieter class but slashed tires. The use of force teaches the use of force. Where parents and teachers use force to get their way, children learn that you can get your way if you're big enough and tough enough.

Part IV
Appendixes

AN APPROACH TO INTER-DISCIPLINARY TEACHING

Procedure	Example
A. Identify those key concepts which are important for students' awareness and growth but which students do not recognize because of their lack of experience (e.g., prejudice, the nines table, power and powerlessness, the human circuiatory system, international balance of payments, body language, the decimal system).	A. Prejudice, racial discrimination, the position of ethnic minorities in American society.
B. Select a concept and determine duration of unit. (The breadth or nar-	B. Racial discrimination: three weeks (five class periods per week).

rowness of the concept must correlate with the amount of time available for its exploration.)	
C. Establish goals (to be augmented or modified later by students).	C. To make white, middle-class, suburban students aware of what it feels like to be always an underdog.
D. Set up situations where students will confront the concept experientially (either through actual encounter or through simulation).	D. Simulation — brown-eyed students get special privileges, blue-eyed students get special handicaps.
E. Explore these experiences through discussion and value-clarifying activities.	E. Discuss feeling and ask for values cards on the experience.
F. Introduce relevant materials from the disciplines.	F. *Black Like Me, Manchild in the Promised Land, Raisin in the Sun, The Merchant of Venice,* descriptions of slave auctions, unemployment statistics broken down by ethnic groups (past as well as present), etc.

Appendix B

A CONVERSATION
AMONG TEACHERS

NOTE: *In January 1973, Edgar C. Alward and Robert C.
Hawley conducted an intensive course entitled "Communica-
tion for Personal and Social Growth" at the Western
Massachusetts Regional Office of the State Department of
Education in Springfield. The sponsor was Westfield State
College. The following is excerpted from a follow-up con-
ference held at the beginning of February 1973.*

GEORGE ELSNER *(social studies teacher, middle school)*:
I've been doing a unit called "Parents and Children" with one
of my seventh grade groups. We're trying to get at whether or
not there really is a generation gap, and if so, what to do
about it. I guess that the first part is sort of a consciousness-
raising business. I showed the film "Claude."[1] It's only three
minutes, and in it there's a boy building something in a little
black box while his parents are around paying him no
attention. Then he throws the switch and they disappear.
That's the end of the film. The kids were really interested,
and we discussed what had happened, and especially what the
boy had done to his parents.

BOB HAWLEY: What do they think happened?

GEORGE: Well, it was funny. Nobody thought that the boy had killed his parents. They really couldn't explain.

ED ALWARD: I wonder if any of the students wished they had their own little black boxes.

GEORGE: Well, I asked them that, and most said they would like to have one just for certain times. Mostly when their parents yell at them or else won't listen. Those seem to be the two things that really bother the kids.

BOB: Maybe because yelling and not listening are two signs that the kids take to mean their parents don't value them as human beings. It means a loss of self-respect.

MARY RIX (*fifth grade teacher*): But aren't there some times when a parent yells at a child because she loves him? I think I do.

BOB: That's right; but it's not the motives of the parent that count here; it's the perception of the child. Yelling apparently fails to communicate the love and respect that the parent may feel.

GEORGE: Then we used the "Marijuana Story" as a follow-up. [See page 180.] I asked the students to rank the five characters in order from the one whose actions they most approved to the one whose actions they least approved. The thing that really bothered them in the story was that the parents wouldn't listen to the youngsters.

ED: That's interesting. I think we find that that kind of not listening is characteristic of teacher behavior in the classroom, too.

GEORGE: Yes, and that reminds me of one more thing. Since I've been taking this course, I've been having my students move their desks into a circle instead of having rows. I'm what they call a "floating teacher," that is, I don't have a room of my own, and so I have them arrange the desks at the beginning of the period and then put them back at the end because the other teachers don't like it that way.

BOB: I wish you could get the other teachers to try it.

GEORGE: The kids were funny the first time I tried it. They thought that they were being rude because at my encouragement they started speaking directly to one another without waiting for me to lead the discussion. But now they really like it. In fact, one day last week I was late getting into a class, and they had already set up the desks in a circle.

BOB: One of the things that I'm hearing is that even though it takes five to ten minutes out of the period to arrange the desks, you feel it's worth it, that is, you get more done in less time.

GEORGE: Oh, yes, very definitely. There's one other thing: I've always enjoyed teaching, but I really look forward to my classes more now. Even though it takes me an extra half-hour a night to prepare.

BOB: That's something that really concerns me. One of the things that we have to keep working on is ways to do some of that planning during the school day so as to prevent teacher burn-out. I mean, you can keep up giving a half-hour extra to your schoolwork for just so long. You've got to leave time for yourself, or you'll wear out too fast.

ED: In many ways, it's like being a beginning teacher all over again. It takes longer to prepare now, but once you get used to it, I think it will take less time. When I started using these methods, I nearly worked myself to death. But now I've sort of developed a rhythm, and some things come more naturally to me.

MARTY CONROY (*seventh grade English teacher*): Well, I

did something that was very simple—*Letter to the Teacher*. [See page 97.] I've been setting aside part of a period every other week for students to write me a private letter. Then I read them, and write something back on each one and return them. It's been very successful. I've gotten to know my students a lot better. When I see them in the hall and say "Hi," I feel that there's more between us than before, that is, we have more things in common. This is one that I didn't let anybody "pass" on. I felt that everybody could have something to say to me. One girl said that it was stupid and then went on to write two pages of very personal and important things that she wanted to say to me.

RUTH HOLMAN (*elementary learning disabilities specialist*): It's too bad that you couldn't write a letter back to each one. They love to receive letters.

MARTY: I've got over a hundred students, so I really can't do that. But I do put a little note on each one.

BOB: That's very important. Something so that they know you've read and understood. Nothing kills that kind of program faster than having those letters disappear so that they don't know whether you've even looked at them or not. The other thing that kills *Letters to the Teacher* dead is if you comment on mechanics, spelling, handwriting, and so forth.

It seems that what we come down to talking about again and again is open communication. What other ways are you using to open up communication in your classes?

MARTY: Well, I've noticed that since I've started sitting on the floor with my kids, they have been much more open. We have some great discussions now.

BOB: You and your children are on the same level. It

seems that just the physical setting has a lot to do with open communication — being on the same level or all sitting in a circle and so on.

LEO ALVARES (*seventh and eight grade English teacher*): We've been doing something in the way of community building that you might call opening communication. Last Monday we made a class telephone directory, and then for their assignment everyone called everyone else. We've been telephoning like crazy. The first night I gave out an assignment over the phone, which was to bring a blindfold and an orange for the next day's class. Then in class we did an activity where everybody picks out his own orange blindfolded. They all got their own oranges back, and then, of course, they ate them. The next night, I sent them home with sealed envelopes. The envelopes contained a copy of "The Marijuana Story" and somebody's phone number to call and try to convince each other about which of the characters did the best thing and so on. On the third night, I asked everybody to watch the same TV program and then to call somebody and discuss it.

BOB: Oh, telephoning, that's a great idea! Did everybody get a call?

LEO: Yes, they worked it out in class so that everybody would get at least one call. And of course they could make as many as they wanted.

ED: Did you have any students who had no phone?

LEO: There were a couple, but they had some kind of access, and that worked out all right. One thing, if you're going to try it: be sure to have a copy of the phone book, because some of the kids can't remember their own numbers.

ED: Here is something that's a product of our technology that can be really useful in teaching. I bet that students learn to listen better over the telephone, too. And yet the telephone is such an ordinary thing that you'd never really think of it for something like that.

BOB: You know, the things we've been talking about are not really very spectacular or elaborate, but I've got a feeling that they make a real difference in the lives of our students, and in our own lives as well.

Notes

1.   "Claude" was produced by Don McLaughlin, distributed by Pyramid Films, Santa Monica, California.

Appendix C

SUGGESTIONS FOR FURTHER READING

Assagiolo, Roberto, M.D. *Psychosynthesis*. New York, Viking Press, 1965. A presentation of the theory and practice of a major school of existential psychotherapy, with an emphasis on the development of the will. Many implications for educators, and some specific applications.

Bach, Richard. *Jonathan Livingston Seagull*. New York, Macmillan Company, 1970. You too can fly!

Brown, George Isaac. *Human Teaching for Human Learning*. New York, Viking Press, 1971. An introduction to confluent education; that is, the combining of affective and cognitive learning. Gestalt oriented. Many useful activities are described.

Glasser, William, M.D. *Schools Without Failure*. New York, Harper & Row, 1969. Presents sound rationale to abolish grading plus some useful alternatives. Also includes an exposition of Glasser's "classroom meeting" technique.

Gordon, W.J.J. *The Metaphorical Way of Learning and Knowing*. Cambridge, Mass., Porpoise Books, 1971. Synectics applied to the classroom. An exciting approach to unlocking the doors of creativity in students.

Greer, Mary, and Rubinstein, Bonnie. *Will the Real Teacher Please Stand Up: A Primer in Humanistic Education*. Pacific Palisades, Calif., Goodyear Publishing Co., 1972. Many activities and some useful theory.

Hawley, Robert C. *Value Exploration Through Role Playing*. New York, Hart Publishing Co., 1974. A variety of formats for role playing and many practical suggestions for their use in the classroom. Special attention to role playing and the development of moral judgment. Naturally, we think this is a super book.

Holt, John. *How Children Fail*. New York, Dell Publishing Co., 1964. An awareness-raising book. Required reading for all parents and teachers.

_____. *What Do I Do Monday?* New York, Dell, 1970. Many useful ideas for classroom teachers.

Jones, Muriel, and Jorgenward, Dorothy. *Born to Win*. Reading, Mass., Addison-Wesley, 1971. A combination of Gestalt Therapy and Transactional Analysis as an aid to understanding behavior and promoting growth. Includes specific techniques for teachers.

Kirschenbaum, Howard, Simon, Sidney B., and Napier,

Rodney, W. *Wad-Ja-Get? The Grading Game in American Education.* New York, Hart Publishing Co., 1971. A novel approach to exposition of the damaging effects of the grading system and what one fictional high school did about it. Excellent annotated bibliography of research on grading.

Maslow, Abraham H. *Motivation and Personality,* 2nd ed. New York, Harper & Row, 1970. Every teacher should memorize this book. One of the cornerstones in humanistic psychological theory.

Overly, Norman V., ed. *The Unstudied Curriculum: Its Impact on Children.* Washington, D.C., Association for Supervision and Curriculum Development, 1970. Many thought-provoking essays including a concise statement by Lawrence Kohlberg of his theory and research in the development of moral judgment.

Perls, Frederick S., M.D., Ph. D. *Gestalt Therapy Verbatim.* Lafayette, Calif., Real People Press, 1969. Transcripts of tapes by Fritz Perls, the founder of Gestalt Therapy. The most useful statement of what Gestalt is all about.

Postman, Neil, and Weingartner, Charles. *Teaching as a Subversive Activity.* New York, Dell Publishing Co., 1969. Argues that education should be a process of challenging the assumptions of society in order to test their validity. Many examples of how teachers can change their classroom behaviors to promote social awareness in their students.

Prince, George M. *The Practice of Creativity: A Manual for Dynamic Group Problem Solving*. New York, Harper & Row, 1970. An exposition of the "Synectic" problem-solving technique — ways to enhance creative problem solving.

Raths, Louis E., Harmin, Merrill, and Simon, Sidney B. *Values and Teaching: Working with Values in the Classroom*. Columbus, Ohio, Charles E. Merrill, 1966. This is the original values-clarification manual. It contains the rationale and a wealth of useful value-clarifying activities.

Rogers, Carl. *Freedom to Learn*. Columbus, Ohio, Charles E. Merrill, 1969. Rogers' manifesto on education. One of the foundations of humanistic education.

Schmuck, Richard A., and Schmuck, Patricia A. *Group Processes in the Classroom*. Dubuque, Iowa, Wm. C. Brown Co., 1971. Recent research and some practical activities to help teachers become more effective facilitators of group processes.

Schrank, Jeffrey. *Teaching Human Beings: 101 Subversive Activities for the Classroom*. Boston, Beacon Press, 1972. Chapters on teaching about drugs, death, and violence, among others. Many references to ways to integrate film and other media into the classroom, with listings of film and other source materials.

Shaftel, Fannie R., and Shaftel, George. *Role-Playing for Social Values: Decision-Making in the Social Studies*.

Englewood Cliffs, N.J., Prentice-Hall, 1967. A basic book on role playing. Especially useful for social studies teachers in grades five through eight.

Simon, Sidney B., Hawley, Robert C., and Britton, David D. *Composition for Personal Growth: Values Clarification Through Writing.* New York, Hart, 1973. Originally designed for English teachers but easily adaptable by any teacher trying to humanize his or her classroom. This book contains a myriad of useful and practical ideas for classroom teachers.

Simon, Sidney B., Howe, Leland W., and Kirschenbaum, Howard. *Values Clarification: A Handbook of Practical Strategies.* New York, Hart, 1972. Chock-full of useful values-clarifying techniques.

Spolin, Viola. *Improvisation for the Theater: A Handbook of Teaching and Directing Techniques.* Evanston, Ill., Northwestern University Press, 1963. *The* book on improvisational theater: full of useful teaching games and insights about how students learn.

Weinstein, Gerald, and Fantini, Mario D., eds. *Toward Humanistic Education: A Curriculum of Affect.* New York, Praeger, 1970. A rationale for affective curriculum with several useful activities. Presents the "Trumpet," a model for integrating concerns, thought, and action.

INDEX

INDEX

Accident Report Worksheet, 113
achievement, evaluating, 224-225
    see also grading
achievement motivation, 33-34,
    37, 83-101
    activities for, 90-101
    feedback and, 94-101
    grading and, 238
    three factors establishing, 84-88
Adjective Rating List, 203-205
Alice in Wonderland, 206
Alter Ego Profile Sheet, 201-202
alternative learning styles, 86-87,
    208-210
alternative search, 42-43
Areas of Concern Questionnaire,
    163-164
August, Dietrich, 246

Beethoven, Ludwig van, 19
behavior control, see discipline

Bergman, David, 245-246
brainstorming, 37-43, 91, 93, 101,
    127, 137, 139, 141, 162, 165,
    166, 171-172, 178, 179, 187,
    207, 212, 213, 215, 225-226,
    231, 242-243
    alternative-search, 42-43
    definition of, 37
    rules of, 38-39
    warm-up, 41-42

Change, see decision making
choice, see decision making,
    forced-choice games, value
    exploration and clarification
class meeting, 49
classroom climate and
    environment, 16-18, 23, 49, 84,
    88-89, 225
"Claude," 261-262
College Board Examinations, 55,

85, 210, 211
communication, 34, 37, 89,
    102-134
    activities for, 111-134
    non-verbal, activities for, 130-
    134
Communication Climate
    Inventory, 128-130
    see also communication
    continuums
communication continuums, 104-
    108, 126, 128-130
Communication Guidelines Sheet,
    124-126
community, characteristics of,
    51-52
community building, 33, 37, 50-
    54, 56-82
    activities for, 56-82
    problems in, 52-54
concerns, student, *see* identifying
    student concerns
concerns, teaching, 33-34, 36-37
Coping Questions Box, 169-171
creative thinking, 19-21
curriculum
    change, 218-219
    social entropy and, 24-26
    see also alternative learning
    styles

Darwin, Charles, 19
decision making, 210-219

activities for, 213-217
Dewey, John, 22
discipline, 83, 253-256
drugs, activities relating to, 42,
    150, 164, 180-183

Eaglebrook School, 246
Educational Facilities Laboratory,
    17
empathizing, *see* interpersonal
    relationships
end values, *see* values
English, activities suitable for
    teaching, 140, 149-151, 154-
    155, 209, 215-216
evaluation, activity for, 242-244
    see also grading

Feedback, 65, 66, 117, 184, 187,
    190, 203, 223-224
    activities, 94-101
    as tool in evaluation, 248
Feedback Form, 96
Feedback Sentence Stem Form, 99
Fiji Islands, 177
focus
    activities for developing
        positive, 227-235
    positive and negative, 184, 224-
    227

forced-choice games, 123, 141,
   155-161
Ford Foundation, 17
Friends Academy, 244

Galileo, 19
Gestalt therapy, 55
Gibb, Jack, 103, 104
goals of class, establishing, 84, 85,
   90-94
Gores, Dr. Harold, 17
grading
   alternatives, 244-251
   competition and, 240-241
   evaluation and, 236-251
   major arguments against, 237-
      241
   negative focus and, 225
group process, observing, 65-70,
   72, 77, 78, 79, 80, 81, 123

Hamlet, 26, 28
Hankwitz, Reed, 244
history, activities suitable for
   teaching, 58, 140, 141, 149-
   151, 154-155, 209, 215-216
How Do You Feel Today?
   Worksheet, 185-186

"I Am the Picture" Worksheet,
   169
"I Believe . . ." Statements, 143-
   144, 183
"I Learned . . ." Statements, 119,
   143-144, 160-161, 183, 185,
   189, 195, 198, 200
identifying student concerns,
   activities for, 161-183
identity forming, activities for,
   183-205
Individual Study Contract, 246,
   249
information processing, 34, 37,
   135-144
   activities for, 75-76, 139-144
interpersonal relationships,
   activities for, 65-82
introducing lessons, 46-47
introjectors, 109, 125

Killer statements, 109-110, 125
Kohlberg, Lawrence, 22

Language, activities suitable for
   teaching, 141, 142-143
learning styles, *see* alternative
   learning styles
Life Auction Catalogue Sheet,
   196-197

Macbeth, 154
Maltz, Maxwell, 219
Marijuana Story, The, 141, 180-182, 262, 265
Maslow, Abraham, 14-15
Master of Ceremonies Instruction Sheet, 192-193
mathematics, activities suitable for teaching, 141, 142-143, 154-155
means values, *see* values
moral judgment, teaching for, 22-24
    see also value exploration and clarification
motivation, *see* achievement motivation

New York City School System, 218-219
non-verbal communication, *see* communication
North Quincy High School, 245

Open-chair role play, 53, 171-175
    class arrangement for, 175
orientation, 33, 36, 45-49
Outward Bound program, 140

People and Places Questionnaire, 229-230
Perls, Fritz, 55
Personal Attribute Worksheet, 233
personal inventories, 61-65, 123, 197-200
    see also identity forming
personal self-contract, 42-44
Personal Self-Contract Form, 44
Piaget, Jean, 22
planning for change, 34, 206-219
    see also decision making
Play Ball Process Sheet, 70-71
positive focus, *see* focus
Postman, Neil, 161
procedures, *see* rules and procedures
process observer, *see* group process
Process Observer Sheet, 67-68
    uses of, 66, 78, 80
Profile Questionnaire, 63
Psycho-Cybernetics, 218

Rank ordering, 101, 123, 124, 126-127, 141, 142, 151-155, 166-167, 182, 183, 188, 190, 194, 196-197, 212, 213, 215, 232
resources, identifying, 208-210
right to pass, rationale for, 55-56
Rogers, Carl, 20
role playing, 23-24, 53, 75-77, 128, 140, 168-169, 171-175, 183, 217

role taking, 22-23
rules and procedures, classroom, 48-49, 84, 86-88
Rules for Rushin' Baseball Sheet, 73-74

teaching concerns, sequence of, 33-34, 36-37
TORI method, 103
Twenty-Things-I-Love-to-Do Sheets, 199-200

Science, activities suitable for teaching, 140, 141-142, 149-151
self-actualization, 14-15
self-concept, 89
  see also identity forming
sensory awareness, activities for, 130-134
"Siamese Baseball, " 72
social studies, activities suitable for teaching, 58, 149-151, 166-167, 215-216
Stanford Achievement Test, 243
Student Grade Analysis, 245-246, 247, 248

Validating rounds, 226-227, 228, 234-235
value exploration and clarification, 34, 37, 145-205
  activities for, 149-205
values
  means vs. end, 25-26, 28
  three steps for working with, 148-149
valuing, elements of, 146-148

Tale of Two Cities, 216
Teacher Self-Evaluation Form, 250-251
Teaching As a Subversive Activity, 161

War and Peace, 26
Weingartner, Charles, 161
whip, 92, 97, 158-159

Yearling, The, 151

INDEX OF ACTIVITIES

Accident Report, 111-113
Address List, 58-59
Adjective Rating List, 202-205
Adverbs, 132
Alter Ego, 200-202
Architects and Builders, 114-115
Areas of Concern Questionnaire,
161-164

Be the Picture, 128
Beauty Contest, 77-78
Big Machine, The, 132-133
Blind Landing, 121-122
Blind Puzzle, 118
Blind Walk, 133-134
Body Language Awareness, 127-
128
Brainstorm and Rank Order, 101
Brainstorming to Teach
Organization, 139
Bridge Building, 78-80

Card Lecturette, 141-142
Catch the Cup, 119-120
Color Profiles, 62
Communication Cards, 115-117
Communication Climate
Inventory, 126-127, 128-130
Communication Guidelines
Rank Order, 124-126
Coping Questions, 169-171
Current Events, 166-167

"Dear Me" Letters, 97-98
Decision Charting, 213-214
Decisions—An Open-Chair
Brainstorm and Role Play,
171-175
Decisions Role Plays, 217
Designated Feedback Person, 101

Evaluation Brainstorming, 242-
244

Feedback Box, 100
Feedback Forms, 95-96
Feedback Sentence Stems, 97,99
Feedback Wall, 100
Focus Listening, 122-123
Force-Field Analysis, 215-216
Forced-Choice Games and Rank
    Orders, 141
Future Questions, 165-166

Goals Dyads, 93
Group Dreams—Round Robin,
    176-177

Here-and-Now Words, 187-188
High-Tension Wire, 140
Hopes, 90-91
Hopes Brainstorm, 91-92
Hopes Whip, 92
How Do You Feel Today?, 184-
    187
Human Knots, 117

I Am the Picture, 167-169
"I Learned . . ." and "I Believe
    . . ." Statements, 143-144
"I Learned . . ." Statements, 160-
    161

Leader and the Led, The, 75-77
Letters to the Teacher, 97
Life Auction, 194-197
Lloyd's of London—Specialized
    Insurance Policies, 177-178

Magic Box, 60-61
Marijuana Story, The, 180-183
Mirror Dance, 131

Name Tags, 56-58

Paper Profiles, 61-62
People and Places Questionnaire,
    227-230
Personal Attributes, 232-233
Photo Profiles, 64
Play Ball, 68-71
Pockets, 178-180
Process Observer, 65-66

Rank Order, 151-155
Role Plays and Simulations, 140
Rushin' Baseball, 71-74

Self-Collage, 64-65
Singing Sam, 59
Skill Rounds, 142-143
Space Ambassadors, 156-158
Support Brainstorm and Letter
   Writing, 230-232

Telegrams, 98
Tinker Toys, 80-82
To Tell the Truth, 190-193
Topic Brainstorm, 93-94
Twenty Things I Love to Do,
   197-200

Validating Rounds, 234-235
Value Cards, 160
Value Voting, 149-151
Value Whips, 158-159

Who Am I?, 188-190
Who Am I?—Who Do You Think
   I Am?, 190

Yes, Robert, No, Susan, 119

ROBERT C. HAWLEY is the author of *Value Exploration Through Role Playing,* and is co-author with Sidney B. Simon and David D. Britton of *Composition for Personal Growth* (both books published by Hart). He has taught for 16 years, at the junior high school, high school, and college levels. He received his doctorate from the University of Massachusetts at Amherst.

ISABEL L. HAWLEY holds a Ph.D. from the University of North Carolina at Chapel Hill. She has been teaching for 15 years, at the high school and college levels.